THE EXPAT'S GUIDE TO JAPAN

JM Hewitt

Christophe, Steve – Thank You

Table of Contents

Introduction

Being an effective manager or leader in Japan requires the same basic principles as in any country. Establish your credibility, engage with your teams, be clear and be fair. It's not rocket science and the points are familiar to anyone already experienced in working with a team of one to a company of thousands.

The issue in Japan is how to effectively do this. You may only have a limited time, possibly a two or three year contract, which can easily translate into enthusiasm, followed by ineffectiveness, followed by frustration, followed by looking forward to your next role anywhere other than Japan.

Things don't have to be like that. It is true that engaging when you don't speak the language may be problematic but there are ways to address this and being clear in a culture where the answer tends to be "yes" simply takes time to learn the warning signs. Establishing credibility comes with not simply knowing your subject but also how to apply that knowledge. Being fair might seem straightforward but potentially not in the context where what is considered "fair" may be subtly different to that which you are used to.

This book has been written, drawing on more than twenty years experience in the corporate world of Japan, to help kick-start the process of being an effective and successful leader here. Having been expatriated from the UK at a few weeks notice to an office in desperate need of an English speaker, I found myself somewhat surprised that no one around me spoke English. May be I should have thought a little about why there was a desperate need for an English speaker in the first place.

This was the start of a very steep learning curve that led through experience in services, automotive, sports and luxury sectors with ultimately the plunge into entrepreneurship and authorship.

In my earlier book, *The Beginner's Guide to Japan*, I cover the issues of simply living in Japan, what's different and why things are the way they are with points as relevant to the expatriate as they are to the non-working spouse and family. This book however is written specifically for the expatriate and addresses some of the pitfalls as well myths around working in Japan.

One of the key principles that is as relevant in that context as it is in this is that *there are no wrongs and rights in Japan, simply differences*. Everyday for the new foreigner can be a challenge, from motivating staff to recognizing the differences in decision processes. It can be a frustrating process but the general wisdom is to change yourself; it's quicker than changing Japan.

That said, as the new executive in the office, there will be continuous examples of areas crying out to you for change however, approaching this from the opinion that something requires improvement is much more effective and satisfying than starting from assuming something is fundamentally wrong. It may seem the most inefficient process ever devised, but there may well be a market force behind it that makes it actually the most efficient in the existing circumstances.

Another key principle is *if you think you understand, you probably don't*. I once followed a heated on-line debate between a person who had recently arrived in Japan and a more seasoned expatriate who had been on the ground for a number of years and was advising caution in taking action too quickly. The new arrival took quite some offence to this and suggested that it was the long-timer who was too slow and that they would shake things up and be successful.

I have no idea what happened in this particular case but have seen many times over the years a new arrival thinking they understand everything around them only to fail at the first hurdle when it becomes obvious they didn't know or realize they were no longer on familiar ground. There is no fixed timeline to how long this acclimatization process will take but as a guideline *a foreigner who realizes they don't understand will be the much more successful than the one who thinks they do*.

This book covers everything from the differences in management style in Japan to the importance of socializing with the staff. It also addresses the question of managing in a crisis, something that affected all of us in the days and weeks that followed the earthquake of March 2011 and the subsequent Fukushima debacle.

When I look back at that time, it seems almost unreal as Tokyo slowly unwound and for a few days appeared to be on the verge of literally dying on its feet. Drawing on that and other experiences, including the destruction of the city of Kobe in 1995, I have also included a straightforward and common sense approach as to how to manage under crisis conditions with six simple and low cost points that could make the difference between success and failure, personal and corporate.

Being a successful leader in Japan can take a little time for a foreigner to acclimatize to and gather their wits around them. But it can be done and done very successfully. They simply need to start from the position that all their previous experience may no longer be relevant. And then take it from there.

An Expat's Cheat Sheet

If there's one part of this book I wish I'd been able to hang on my wall in the days and months after I first arrived in Japan it would be the following *forty seven habits of successful expats in Japan*. This is by no means an exhaustive list of key concepts, tips and thoughts but it provides a solid base on where to start.

Asking any long-term expatriate to write their own set of rules that would have helped them to success in their early days, each time there will be a different list. However, show this to a long-term expat and more than likely the majority would also make it onto their favorites list as well.

The interesting thing about this is how it will change in meaning over time. An initial review will undoubtedly lead to an element of agreement but potentially some of the more important elements will appear at first completely innocuous. It's only when the actual experience hits you head-on that you realize the underlying meaning of the point.

This book explains and illustrates each of the points below and aims to provide the reader with the understanding on how to avoid the pitfalls that await and how to turn a situation to their own advantage. At first many of the points will simply make you smile and may appear self-evident or an excessive generalization. Over time though you may come back and tick off each point in turn and, if this book has done its work properly, you'll have been more successful in the process.

Forty Seven Habit of Successful Expats in Japan

1   Remembering it's the same skill set to be successful in Japan, it's the experience that's different;

2   When you think you understand, think again;

3   The expat is the center of attention, whether they know it or not;

4   It's not wrong, it's just different;

5   Ask first, speak second;

6   It's the team in public, the individual in private;

7   Avoid negative questions;

8   The successful expats realize they don't understand earlier than the unsuccessful ones;

9   It's all about the stakeholder, not the shareholder;

10   Business relations are personal not corporate;

11   Keiretsu. It's one big family;

12   You don't need to do the deal to make the friend;

13   Japan is not China, the same as France is not Mexico;

14   The parallel market is all about economics, but it can help you find your consumer;

15   The boss should be a communicator, nationality is less important;

16   Decisions: there's more than one way to reach the conclusion;

17   Japanese titles are more important to Japanese staff than English titles;

18   "Apology" is the wrong word. It's a recognition of circumstance rather than acceptance of guilt or reflection of remorse;

19   Implementing something new is a question of willpower. It can be done;

20   The bonenkai is an important concept. It's not a Christmas party;

21   If no one is waiting for the nijikai, it's you, not them;

22   The "Break" is the expats "Get-Out-of-Jail-Free" card;

23   Bonuses are not necessarily bonuses, they're often expected;

24   There's data privacy and then there's everything about you;

25   Sometimes you just won't understand; you just won't;

26   Yes can mean "yes", "no" or "huh?";

27   Offshore contracts save the expat and the company money;

28   A joint venture is either a legal requirement or fear of the dark;

29   The greeting is important, do it once and do it well;

30   Your word is your bond; paper comes later;

31   Full visual check, shoes, socks, wallet;

32   Just because someone speaks English doesn't mean they understand English;

33   Anything can be explained in three sentences;

34   Confirm, confirm, confirm!

35   Follow-up, follow-up, follow-up!

36   Lose your cool and engagement turns to containment;

37   Check the Japanese with someone who is Japanese;

38   Foreigners explain, Japanese demonstrate;

39   Nothing travels faster than confidential information;

40   It's more efficient to invest a little time in understanding Japan than a lot of time in learning Japanese;

41   Information can be translated, emotion can't;

42   People don't learn English in an English class;

43   Never tell a joke through a translator;

44   Remember overtime is a chronic disease;

45   Crises: Prepare, People First, Communicate, Be Flexible, Act Quickly, Stay Positive;

46   If you don't like it don't complain, change;

47   There's a reason for everything. Including why there are forty-seven habits of successful expats in Japan.

Corporate Japan – a different style

In western countries, the members of the Board of Directors of a company have a fiduciary duty to shareholders of that company and must act at all times in their best interests. Indeed they may be liable to prosecution if they act in any way otherwise. Although also a legal requirement, in practice this is not necessarily so in Japan.

Although legally the directors must act in the best interests of the shareholders, culturally companies are expected to be acting in the interests of all stakeholders, not just the shareholders. The loosely defined term of stakeholder is considered to include the employees of the company, the community within which the company operates and, to a certain degree, its customers and suppliers.

Companies in Japan therefore could be considered to have different priorities to those in the West. Stability is highly valued at a macro and a micro level as are the relationships between companies that have developed over years or decades. The employee who makes waves will be encouraged to toe the line and a customer in trouble may be supported until they are back on their feet.

The tightly interwoven keiretsu system of interlocking shareholdings, developed to circumvent the post-war requirement to dismantle the zaibatsu system of a small number of immensely powerful companies and corporate groupings, is in reality breaking down in the modern era. Twenty years of economic stagnation and financial collapse has led to some rationalization of the corporate landscape.

Business – the importance of being earnest

The importance and implications of good business relationships cannot be over-emphasized. In Japan this means the personal relationships between the individuals in two companies and not just the abstract concept of the relationship between the companies themselves. It is a general rule of most societies that people tend to work with others they know and like. Although still the case, the difference arises though that, in general in Japan, people will not work with people they do not like or trust.

If you are finding your business is struggling it may not be due to competition or product offering, it may well be the state of the relationship between your company or predecessor and the market. Significant efforts are made at all levels by Japanese executives to ensure good personal relationships with business partners and this is as critical for the expat as for anyone else.

As a foreigner working in Japan you will need to invest significant time and effort into this process. It's not something you can delegate or ignore and will mean sacrifice of many evenings with the family in the cause of dinner with the client. Your business will grow on the back of a good personal relationship and it will suffer from the effects of a poor one. Invest the time, join the dinners and the golf days, know your counterparts on a personal basis and it will reflect positively on the entire business in the long term. *Business relationships are personal rather than corporate in Japan.*

International and Domestic Companies

Gaishikei is the word used for the subsidiary of a foreign company operating in Japan where as kaisha, although simply meaning "company" carries and inference of being a domestic Japanese company. The management style and internal culture of each have traditionally been significantly different even to the extent that a Japanese employee choosing to work for a foreign gaishikei may have difficulty returning to the Japanese corporate world. It will generally be considered that they made an unusual career choice and may well be viewed with what amounts to an element of suspicion.

This is actually a significant advantage for foreign companies as the talent pool that can be recruited from is essentially separate from that of domestic companies and therefore there is little competition between the two. Additionally, gaishikei can take an advantage in recruiting women, normally marginalized in Japanese companies, where their education is equal to their male counterparts and their career opportunities and resulting motivation can be significantly higher.

A good example of the difference in philosophy between the domestic and foreign companies lies in the recruitment process. A foreign company will have a vacancy and recruit to fill it; a domestic company will recruit first and subsequently assign the individual to their new career path.

Within a foreign company it is normal that an individual new recruit will have a good understanding of why they have joined the company, what their role will be and how their career should progress. These aspects of choosing where you decide to work seem relatively basic to someone who has worked in a Western culture but are not necessarily so in Japan. New recruits straight out of university will often arrive en masse on day one and be told what their new career is going to be with little or no discussion. Especially for women, this might vary from being a trainee bond dealer to the office tea lady.

I once challenged a company I worked with as to why women were paid approximately 20% less than their male counterparts for the same work. I received a number of explanations all of which were, in effect, an attempt to cover over a traditional working practice. Once I demonstrated that the women were more loyal, on average staying longer at the company, incurred higher overtime and scored comparable results on annual appraisals, there seemed little reason for the differential in pay. Interestingly it was the HR team that were most against the proposal for equality but the foreign management were very supportive. And eventually, the women were paid the same.

Keiretsu – the post-war ties that bind

During the Meiji restoration in the second half of the nineteenth century, the Japanese economy was rapidly modernized by focusing capital into large, family owned industrial behemoths. These were called the *zaibatsu* and dominated the economic landscape and the cores remain recognizable even today in the groupings of the likes of the big four Mitsui, Mitsubishi, Yasuda and Sumitomo.

Interestingly, Honda was also one of the original zaibatsu but one of the Honda ladies offended the wives of a number of others who then proceeded to orchestrate a run on the Bank of Taiwan, owned by Honda, and crippled it to the extent the group never really recovered. Be aware of who you offend in Japan!

Post-war, the allied forces were concerned that the zaibatsu represented effective monopolies in their individual areas and essentially disbanded them by eliminating holding companies such that groupings were significantly harder to form. In reality the concern was well founded as between them the zaibatsu not only controlled significant portions of the economy but that of the political structure as well.

The prohibition of holding companies enacted in 1947 remained in place until 1997 when it was relaxed to some extent and thus defined an alternative economic structure for Japanese corporate entities to the common grouping structures in the West.

The concept of an industrial grouping however remained familiar and ingrained, even if the process of creating them had been outlawed. To resolve this the groupings effectively re-invented themselves by each member company holding a small percentage in each other. These groupings are today called *keiretsu*.

The structure of a keiretsu tends to be similar in most cases. At the center is a bank and a large trading house with multiple companies interlocked around these. The group will include manufacturing as well as financial services and look internally to be self-sufficient before considering looking outside the group for any additional requirements. Still today, Mitsubishi and Sumitomo feature strongly in the keiretsu structure as do Mitsui and the Fuyo Group that were also originally zaibatu.

This may seem irrelevant but if a company trades with a member of one keiretsu it will soon find that it's banking relations are being focused into the same group as will insurance and other requirements. Subtly the grouping will begin to provide all the necessary services to a new foreign business in Japan.

Balancing this can sometimes be difficult in the sense of the relationship with the original contact.

Usually though group policies require balance between suppliers and if this is the case, it's perfectly acceptable to let your new partners know that you are unable to work with just one grouping. They will understand and recognize that you also understand.

One interesting point on keiretsu is that they also mostly have an affiliation with one brewery or another. If you find yourself being invited to dinner by a senior member of one of the keiretsu, it is always a good idea to know which beer brand they control. You can then order that type of beer and trash the others and your host will be delighted. Just remember Sapporo and Yebisu beers belong to the Fuyo group, Asahi to Sumitomo and Kirin to Mitsubishi. Enjoy your dinner.

Cross shareholdings – a vote of confidence

Although the days of the keiretsu appear numbered, though in terms of decades rather than years, the concept of a low value cross shareholding remains relatively common. The idea being that when a new business relationship begins it is only polite to purchase a small holding in a new business partner. The value of this can be relatively insignificant in financial terms, a few million yen rather than a few million dollars. The point is the principle of stating you have such faith in your new partner that you would like to hold a small number of their shares.

Almost all listed companies in Japan will do this and conversely look for partners to acquire stock in them too. The point here though is that it is also just as acceptable not to acquire a share holding. For most foreign companies, the purchase of stock, no matter how small, is something that is likely to raise questions at the head office level. And as shareholdings must be reported on the balance sheet, it is something the head office will become aware of.

Although there may be quite some significant pressure to take a stake in a new partner, the reality is that Japanese companies understand this is not considered normal business for foreign companies. New business partners are looking for a good relationship and are not set on creating a problem. A simple "I'm sorry, much as I'd like to, our corporate policy won't allow for that" is more than enough to satisfy face and maintain a good relationship. *You don't need to do the deal to make the friend.*

Multi-branded Retail – it's really not China

Japan is a country of multi-branded retail similar to America or many parts of Europe. It's dissimilar though to China or Korea which are predominantly mono-branded retail and require entirely different business techniques and strategies.

In a mono-branded environment, it is the brand that carries the power. If the retailer isn't happy with the conditions, they have little option but to comply as they are unable to switch brands without changing the store design or supplier. And if they did then they would simply be back to square one but with a different brand and a weaker bank account.

In a multi-branded environment this is reversed. The retailer essentially holds the power as they always have the option of re-directing orders to a different brand. The consumer doesn't mind if the store is 20% brand A and 10% brand B; but brand B does.

This becomes a very visible issue in both pricing and other terms of trade. If a brand decides that it will implement a no-returns policy, it is effectively transferring the inventory risk from itself to the retailer. In a mono-branded environment this is clearly possible as the retailer has no choice. However, in a multi-branded environment, the retailer will more than likely switch the balance to a different player if they are unwilling to accept the higher level of risk undertaken.

Although this seems relatively obvious when, it often it requires some discussion on the subject. Especially if someone is from a mono-branded background.

In the current environment there is a considerable focus on China and you may find yourself in a discussion that is not making particular sense until you account for the fact that the counterpart may only have experience with, and exposure to, that market. It is always worth keeping in the back of your mind that, without laboring the point, this isn't China, it's Japan.

The Grey Market – annoyance and opportunity

The parallel, or grey, market in Japan for genuine product is distracting and disruptive for a number of reasons. Not only is your brand appearing in the wrong distribution channels but you are just as responsible from a consumer protection perspective as if you'd sold the product yourself. The parallel market is big and real and for luxury brands can represent a significant proportion of their business in Japan.

The market, where genuine product is finding its way into Japan through unofficial channels, arises predominantly for economic reasons rather than lack of access to the product itself. Once the mark-up from a home market exceeds 40%, the economics begin to work. It becomes possible for an importer to purchase product in-store overseas, import, retail the item and still maintain a viable profit margin. This is why Louis Vuitton limits purchases in flagship stores in Europe to a few items. More than this and they can be relatively sure it will soon find its way into the grey market in Japan.

Walking through the streets of Shimbashi in central Tokyo there are a number of outlets retailing genuine product that has been sourced from anywhere except the legitimate retailer. And, as there is little the brand can do to control this market as it is perfectly legal, the issue is how to control the supply. The retailers are not claiming to be the brand and the product is retailed without using the brand logo. Nothing illegal there.

The supply can arise from a number of sources and there are trading houses dedicated to managing the import and distribution of leading brands. Product released into the market in the US will take a matter of days to arrive into the parallel market in Japan.

A quick review of CRM data will show a small number of excessively large purchases outside Japan. One luxury handbag brand found that the top customers in their home market were purchasing over 3,000 units a year but also returning 1,000 of these.

Effectively the purchaser was buying through the home market Factory Outlet channel, reviewing each item for quality control purposes and then shipping the good product to Japan through consolidators. The product was being bought legally and legitimately through the brands own retail channels in one market and, through price arbitrage, being profitably retailed in another.

Pricing in each market is clearly a question of brand identity and positioning and so if the retail price in Japan is greater than 40% higher than the retail in another market, it is going to happen. The key question is what to do about it.

The first point is to identify the extent of the issue. By mapping outlets across Japan where the brand is found it becomes possible to identify where the demand for the product is being satisfied through the parallel market. You may find, for instance, that in Sapporo you have two of your own retail stores whereas there may be twenty or more parallel doors.

This clearly tells you that there is a demand in that area that is not being satisfied for one reason or another, potentially pricing, but also due to simple accessibility. Opening a Factory Outlet store may be the solution to this.

Parallel buyers who purchase at retail rather than on-line tend not to be brand loyal but are very much price aware. Provide them the product at a price they are satisfied with and the consumer will almost always purchase through a legitimate channel rather than a parallel store.

A more extreme approach in the case of significant supply into the market is to actually talk to the distributors themselves. These businesses are always looking for a steady, reliable supply. A number of brands over the years have adopted the approach of actually working with these channels. Rather than trying to control the product they are effectively accepting that the parallel market is going to happen and so the best approach is to manage it rather than trying to beat it, or worse still, ignore it.

The approach is to agree with the importer that you will provide steady product but you will decide what the product is and when they will receive it. No more three-day lag between launching a flagship item and it appearing in the parallel channel. In return the importer must agree to only source product through you and if they are found to be sourcing from elsewhere then the supply will be terminated.

The incentive for the importer is that their supply chain has been significantly simplified and supply guaranteed and that the disruption to this will be so extreme if they violate the agreement that it is not worth their while to do so.

As a result of using rather than suffering the parallel market, brands can not only identify where they are under-represented but can also control the flow of their product in the unofficial channels that are going to arise due to pricing differentials between markets. Better the devil you know as it were.

Although the thought of working with, rather than against, the parallel channel may make some recoil in horror, the issue is that there is a genuine demand for this product at a lower price than it is being officially retailed for in the market.

This demand is not simply going to vanish just because the brand doesn't appreciate it, it will be out there and unless satisfied directly, it will be satisfied indirectly. If you remain unconvinced, take a visit to a Bic Camera store and ask yourself where all those luxury products came from. Not all are through a process of managed supply, but some are.

The parallel market can also provide a market indicator as to pricing and distribution. In the instance that parallel product retails at a premium to authorized channels this suggests that either the official pricing is too low or demand is not being satisfied due to lack of access (physical or virtual). This was actually the case recently for a US children's wear brand which found its core products being retailed on-line by third parties at a higher price point that in its own stores. The conclusion being, whether a brand likes it or not, the parallel market should not be ignored.

One final interesting point on the flow of product into the parallel channels is a uniquely Japanese situation that arises from the hostess clubs rather than international import. Hostess bars are common ground for businessmen who fall for the old routine of "she must really like me" (if ever you have a friend who says that, remind them it's just her job).

The businessman will over time develop their favorite hostess in a club and at some point she will lead him into the discussion of her favorite brand. For example, she may say that Louis Vuitton has released a new bag and that she thinks they're wonderful. The punter, in a vain attempt to gain her pleasure, will purchase the bag and present it to her as a gift.

Each night she then plays the same game with each of her regulars. By the end of the week she may now have several identical Louis Vuitton bags, all but one of which she sells to a parallel import retailer, making a significant sum in the process.

The reason why it's important for her to be specific in identifying which bag is the one she adores at the moment is so that she can show the one she keeps to each of each of her customers and tell him that's the one he bought specially for her. She loves it and always carries it around. The punter is flattered and happy and the girl has made a little spare cash. Everybody wins.

Does Japan play by the rule of law?

Yes. And no. Japan is a law abiding, rules based society, almost all of the time. Once an agreement is reached or contract signed, all parties will stand by it to the letter. However, when it comes to directives by the government a second element called *window guidance* comes into play. This is where the government doesn't actually enact legislation but provides, often unwritten, guidance as to what a company should and should not do.

Although a company may be acting perfectly legally and be totally within its rights, contravening window guidance will have an effect. The usual first stage will be the triggering of a corporate tax audit which in its own right shouldn't be a problem if the company has been complying with tax law. However this can be onerous on the individuals who have not only their regular day job to perform but now have to double down to help with the audit. After that it could be an FTC raid, a withholding tax audit or one of a number of excessive compliance requirements. When given, it's a good idea to take the guidance.

The second element of lack of transparency is the refusal by both tax and customs authorities to provide written, positive confirmation of an opinion. At the end of an audit they will tell you what you have been doing wrong but will not provide written confirmation that what you have been doing is actually right. The problem is that this leaves the door open for the next audit to challenge the opinion of the previous one and a whole line of discussion is re-opened for review.

It is important to emphasize though that Japan as a country, and Japanese people as a culture, overwhelmingly follow the rule of law. Corruption, except in a small number of rather spectacular cases, is minimal to the extent it is not something to be considered. Obviously this is unlike a number of other countries in Asia where it is necessary to consider all aspects of a deal and not simply the contractual ones.

Should the president be a foreigner?

Among the most successful and inspirational executives I've both met and worked for in Japan have been ones who spoke not a word of Japanese.

And amongst the least effective and most disruptive ones have been any number who spoke excellent Japanese. My conclusion, good executives are good executives whether they speak Japanese or not.

This is an old dilemma for all foreign brands in Japan and tends to be a pendulum swing as opinion at the head office cycles back and forth. The questions arise around not simply skill set and experience but around language, culture and the understanding of the Japanese consumer. But rarely do they revolve around the question of vertical communication. Everyone tends to overlook this point until it is specifically brought to their attention.

The confidence a global business has in its international subsidiaries is driven not simply by quarterly results and the issues above but to a significant degree by the communication lines between the two. Small and simple misunderstandings can grow to being major obstacles to confidence and credibility.

By definition it is the foreign head office that will decide the president of a company and it is the foreign head office that will decide if the time is up and change is needed.

Small misunderstandings over long distances, time zones and regular but not daily contact can lead to mistrust and a breakdown of this necessary confidence. Alternatively, small misunderstandings down the length of a corridor can be managed and resolved simply by walking into someone's office and talking.

The success of the local president is not simply defined by the results but by managing global relationships. Anyone who can do both can be successful in Japan. However manage only one and they'll be looking for a new job sooner than they may realize.

I once worked with a foreigner who spoke reasonably good Japanese but always stayed with English when it came to meetings. Talking to him about this he explained it was a tactic he'd learned many years before. If he switched to working in Japanese, especially in relation to discussions with third parties, he was not so much facilitating the meeting as giving up his most prized asset, thinking time.

There is a reasonable case to be made that having this extra card in your hand is a strategic advantage and therefore a foreigner as the president, whether or not they speak Japanese, is at an advantage from the start. They have the ability to take the time to assess a situation more thoroughly than one who is a native speaker.

The fashion of whether to have Japanese or foreign presidents is exactly that, a fashion. With the required support infrastructure for a foreigner the cost is undoubtedly going to be higher than for a local hire. However if one can grow the business at twice the rate of the other, it's actually the opportunity cost that is the more important measure.

This is a pendulum and tends to swing with the economic conditions of the day. In a down turn the foreigners are recalled home to be replaced by lower cost local hires. In some cases this is extremely successful but in many a frustration builds over time due to the small communication issues and eventually, when conditions allow, the pendulum will swing back and someone the head office is comfortable with will be re-introduced. Those unused to working with Japanese management often construe mis-communication as inability; those small nuances can be more significant than meets the eye.

The decision process – circles and corners

You may have heard stories from people who have visited Japan that Japanese people can take forever to make a decision and have a habit of discussing everything in intense detail beforehand and often afterwards. This is actually true and it's a process which can be extremely frustrating in the Western context as it appears time is being wasted and nothing is being achieved. But not everything is what it seems.

The reality of the situation is actually very different and it's important to recognize this. The Japanese approach to decision making is an all-inclusive one. All parties, as far as practically possible, will be included in a discussion and the issue will be reviewed from multiple different angles. No one individual will stand out and argue for a specific action plan until eventually, and by mutual consent, everyone will agree on the approach and then all work together to achieve a successful outcome. In one go. Aligned.

This review and discussion process is frustrating to foreigners at first and it does appear that nothing is happening, especially when you neither speak the language nor have the Japanese experience in taking this approach. The important point is, that once a decision has been made, everyone is acting in unison and the end result may be achieved very quickly indeed.

Compare this to the typical Western approach to decision making. An objective is stated, a decision is made and an action plan is implemented. Then someone notices something is not working properly or that there might be a better approach to the problem. A new decision is made, the action plan is updated and everyone starts pulling in a different direction. This is then repeated time and again until finally a result is achieved.

Both approaches probably actually take about the same time from inception to completion. However the Japanese approach can be extremely frustrating to a foreigner when nothing appears to be happening. Conversely the Western approach can be extremely disconcerting to Japanese as people rush to implement plans that haven't been fully thought through. Ultimately, both systems have been proved to work, and the most effective will be dependent upon circumstance. Just don't assume nothing is happening. Although it may be.

Japanese titles – exactly who looks up to whom

In the western environment, titles tend to be organized to some degree in a vertical manner understandable mainly within the company itself. Who is to say whether an Executive Vice President in one company is senior or junior to a Senior Vice President in another. And to a large extent many would ask, "who cares?".

However, in the Japanese environment, there is a strict hierarchy of titles, universally understood and followed. The title is more important in Japanese business than in western business as it defines the language of a conversation. The senior person literally is able to use a different vocabulary to the junior and the junior must be careful what he or she says or offence will be taken.

It is common in a western company in Japan for this aspect to be overlooked. A business card will typically have English on one side and Japanese on the other. Foreigners tend to only look at the English side of the card and may completely miss that the Japanese side may be subtly different. To a Japanese employee the only thing that matters is the Japanese title and so they may be unconcerned by any differences, just as long as the Japanese title reflects their position in the broader scheme of business.

It's important then, that when the inevitable re-organization takes place, just as much effort is put into ensuring the Japanese titles are correct as the English language ones. Or you may just find you've promoted someone to be your boss and you never noticed it happening.

The key titles that are used in the Japanese context are:

Kaicho, the Chairman of the Board. Although in unlisted companies in the West it may seem unusual to recognize (or even be aware of) who is actually chairman, as this may be little more than a title of convenience, within the Japanese context this remains an extremely important position and is recognized with due deference and respect. You don't argue with the kaicho as it were.

Shacho, the President of the company. This is used as a general term for the most senior executive position within the business. Essentially the day-to-day decision maker where the English title would be Country Manager, President or CEO.

Fukushacho, the Vice President. "Fuku-", in any context, simply refers to "vice-" or "deputy". In some instances, for example when bringing into the business an heir-apparent to the president, it may also symbolize the person is seen to be associated with the President's department rather than any other area of the company.

Bucho, Department Head or Division Manager. Bucho enters something of a grey area when translated into English. Effectively it is the most senior position below an executive position in a company and may or may not hold a position on the management board. Within the corporate entity it holds significant status and tends to represent the person who has contributed to the success of the business over a long period of time and therefore risen to the rank of senior personnel with a complete department under their stewardship.

Jicho, Deputy Division Manager. This is the position that directly reports to the Bucho and will be next in line for the promotion when the appropriate time comes. The point here being that, although they are knowledgeable and experienced in their role, their time hasn't quite come yet.

Kacho, manager. Kacho is effectively a junior managerial title denoting that the person has responsibility for individual staff underneath them. It's the first rung on the ladder of management.

Shain, staff or employee. Pronounced shai-iin, this represents any staff without managerial responsibility. They are the general employee of the company.

There are a number of additional titles interspersed between these however these are the most commonly used within a company and probably the only ones that Japanese staff would expect a foreign manager to understand and recognize.

The titles though are important across Japanese industry as a whole. Between companies they will be a reasonable benchmark of someone's position, experience and status and can be considered in this light. At the time of a re-organization or re-assignment of titles, the local staff will be significantly more concerned and focused on their Japanese title than on their English language one.

This is not only due to the effect it can have on career prospects if moving between companies but also on such innocuous issues as how their friends and colleagues perceive them even to the extent of how a family may assess their success in a career path.

If Japanese titles are being re-assigned it will take the time and effort to carefully consider the structure and nature of Japanese titles. There will be more discussion and distress over this issue than almost any other within a company.

The Apology – but I didn't do anything wrong!

Irrelevant. Especially if you are in a senior management position, you may find yourself in the situation of needing to provide an apology in certain circumstances. This may seem inappropriate or even legally questionable from a foreigner's point of view however the situation may require it in Japan.

The key issue to note though is that, unlike in Western culture where an apology carries an admittance of guilt, remorse and responsibility, in the Japanese context, *an apology is simply a recognition of a situation* and a statement of wanting to conscientiously try harder in future to avoid the situation arising again.

Counter intuitively, an apology is not an admission of guilt but is a vital step in the process of reconciliation in Japan and you may find that, against all your better judgment and experience, it is necessary and results in a quick and acceptable resolution to all.

Without an apology a situation may quickly gain unnecessary momentum and spiral out of control. For example, in 1982 there was a fire at the Hotel New Japan in central Tokyo. 33 people died in what was one of Japan's worst postwar urban disasters however the manager of the hotel refused to formally apologize stating that he was not responsible for the fire or the resulting loss of life. And he wasn't.

This would seem the appropriate course of action in western business. However, as a result, the burnt out shell of the building remained in prime real estate in Tokyo for the next seventeen years as no contractor could be found willing to redevelop the site. All because the manager simply refused to apologize.

Recently a young, married television actress was caught in the midst of an affair. Her management told her to apologize but she refused and her career is now over. Similarly when a Japanese skater at the Vancouver Olympics only achieved the silver medal, her parents felt it necessary to apologize on national television for their daughter's failure. In Western culture it would seem almost bizarre to apologize but not in Japan.

The only reason this appears utterly unwarranted to a non-Japanese is the key meaning of *an apology being a recognition of the situation rather than an acceptance of guilt and reflection of remorse.*

If you find yourself in the situation of needing to provide an apology, work closely with your Japanese colleagues on developing suitable wording, bite you tongue and get it over with. It will lead to a positive result and a rapid resolution to whatever the issue may have been. It does not imply you are guilty of any wrongdoing or are accepting responsibility for any act. It's simply a recognition that something happened and that in future it is the general desire of everyone to try their best to ensure it doesn't happen again irrespective of whether the situation was wrong or right in the first place. "Apology" is simply the wrong word.

The Bonenkai – it's really not a Christmas Party

This one is always difficult to explain to the head office outside Japan. The *bonenkai* is the year-end corporate event. In some cases it may be held with all employees for just a couple of hours, in some cases it might be on a department basis and go on all night.

However, even though it's in December, it has a very different purpose to the office Christmas Party (Christmas Day is a regular work day in Japan by the way) and plays an important part in corporate culture. In essence, the bonenkai is the last official time to complain about anything that happened during the year. If you're still hung up on something it's time to get it off your chest. And the agreement is, if you don't complain then, you never will in the future. It draws a very clear line under the year and allows people to move on and focus on the future. The key issue is that a bonenkai is a ritualized moment to clear the air. Speak now or forever hold your peace, as it were. It is important and not the moment to be finding cost reductions. It's really not a Christmas party.

The Nijikai – literally the second party

It would be a rare evening indeed if everyone went home directly after the bonenkai (or any other evening event). Usually it has already quietly been arranged for somewhere to go after the first event has run its course.

This is called the *nijikai,* which literally translates as "second time meeting". There'll be another bar or a karaoke box around the corner where the manager is expected to take his team and spend some more time talking and enjoying the evening.

There's a good overall indicator of how well you're settling in at the new office because if there is no one waiting outside the first party, you probably have something to work on.

The nijikai has an element of being for the people who would like to enjoy the evening whereas the earlier event tends to have an air of obligation. For the hardcore element of the team, once the nijikai is over, this is purely an excuse to head straight on for the *sanjikai,* the "three times party"!

This can obviously continue into the early hours but attending a nijikai will please the team who may have gone to significant lengths to organize even a simple event during bonenkai season. Enjoy the time with them, something interesting always comes out of it.

Party Duties – what to do of an evening

For everyone attending the bonenkai, or any other event, there are a few issues to be prepared for. There will be an opening speech and a closing ceremony. The person giving them is usually selected on the spot. Just be prepared with a few choice words, keep it short and keep it upbeat (especially if it is the opening speech as everyone will be politely waiting to start!).

Praise the team as a whole but it's always a good idea to avoid selecting individuals for special recognition. You'll embarrass them rather than earn their appreciation. *Individual praise is much more effective and appreciated in private.*

In the opening speech there is always the *kampai* (the toast), marking the opening of festivities. Technically, no one is supposed to drink before this (so if you've been given the heads up that you're delivering it, don't be late!)

Also, you may want to confirm how many people are expected to be there. I was once asked to deliver a kampai at an event dinner and, expecting about twenty people, was surprised to find approximately 1,500 standing waiting for my elegant words.

The kampai is the moment when the opening speech reaches its final moments. Everyone has a full glass (make sure you have one) and they all raise their glasses together and everyone shouts kampai on the lead of the speaker. Then spontaneous clapping will break out and the party begins. The trick is getting your glass out of your hand fast enough to join the applause.

The closing is a whole different matter. There are two elements to this. First there will be an actual speech, which you may be asked to give. Again, keep it short, explain to the team they've been wonderful to work with and what a great job they've done for the year. Say thank you and then give a slight bow.

What comes next is everyone will rise to their feet, glasses down, and the ceremonial lead will open their arms, palms up, and start a ritualistic clap that everyone joins in. A quick search of YouTube will show you the idea but if you're new to it, politely defer to one of the senior members of the team. This is the official end of the evening and then it's off to the nijikai.

The Shinnenkai – The New Year's Party

The *shinnenkai*, or New Year's Party, is a much lower key affair than the bonenkai but should still occur at the beginning of each year. Although referred to as a party, it is usually more of a speech to the staff and best wishes for the following year. It will be held on or around the first working day of the year. A key difference to the bonenkai is that it would be unusual to invite external guests to the shinnenkai.

All employees will be called together and the senior person present will say a few words of encouragement and then everyone will toast the occasion with a beer or sake.

This is much more of a ceremonial event than a social one and the beer tends to be kept to a minimum. It may even happen first thing in the morning rather than in an evening. One nice touch that can be added is the breaking of a sake barrel. All the senior staff will stand around the barrel and break the lid together with mallets.

Everyone will clap, the staff will enjoy a glass of sake before returning to work, and the wooden cups (*masu*) can act as a nice souvenir for everyone. One word of warning though, don't stand too close to the barrel when you hit it. Someone always hits too hard and sake sprays over those unaware of what is about to happen. The colorful odor of sake will be with you all day and it's a day you'll often be visiting clients.

The shinnenkai is an important ceremony for the company to try and attend. And, more to the point, it's a memorable moment with the team.

The Break – your "Get Out of Jail Free" card

As already highlighted, in Japan there is a wonderful tradition that a not inconsiderable amount of work and communication actually occurs outside the office in the evenings. Drinking and socializing with colleagues is part and parcel of working in Japan. This can obviously lead in some instances with a few too many beers occurring.

To avoid the crushing feeling of embarrassment the next day when facing their colleagues, Japan has developed a wonderful concept called *The Break*. You may actually hear *"breaku, breaku"* being shouted in some instances but what it means is that whatever happens after that moment is off limits for the future. Even if they were dancing on the tables the night before, no one is going to mention it and it will have been effectively erased from everyone's memories.

To re-assure the more hesitant new starters though, no matter what a foreigner gets up to in an evening, I remain yet to be proved wrong that my Japanese colleagues couldn't be one up on them.

One important aspect to the concept of the break is to remember that it applies to everyone, yourself included. It is generally considered poor form to raise the subject of the night before, even if it was a few weeks before and even if it was hysterical. And by keeping the confidence, you become a closer part of the team overall.

The Retirement Allowance – Still defined benefit

The national pension scheme in Japan, when the records have not actually been lost, is a relatively Scrooge like affair. In many cases it's not generally considered sufficient for someone to actually live on, let alone maintain a reasonable standard of living. As a result, the corporate retirement allowance is an important aspect of the remuneration system.

In general, all companies and employees on domestic contracts, must contribute to the national Social Insurance Scheme which is a pay-as-you-go national pension scheme. However, to be able to recruit new employees, almost all companies also offer a retirement package that is non-transferable and pays out when an employee leaves the company. In essence it's a leaving bonus.

Transferable 401K's remain relatively rare in Japan. As a result a typical package is maintained as a liability on the corporate balance sheet rather than as an investment in the equivalent of a pension fund. This has become more ingrained as the stock market has continued to underperform over the last two decades.

The form of the benefit will be defined in the corporate work rules and will be a function of the years worked and the final salary. This will then have a multiplier incorporated that will account for whether the individual is leaving for personal or corporate reasons.

If for corporate reasons the individual receives a greater payout than if they leave of their own accord. Note, therefore, it is a defined benefit scheme in essence rather than a defined contribution scheme. And employees clearly prefer it that way.

This benefit to the individual can clearly represent a significant cost to the company and is necessarily accrued accordingly. However, if it is removed, the company will quickly find that recruitment has become significantly more difficult and that the caliber of individuals joining may not be the same standard as in the days when it was included. It becomes a necessary, though deferred, cost of business in Japan.

Commutation Allowance – but not for you

The daily travel to and from the office cannot only be time consuming (there's no look of surprise when anyone says their daily commute is two hours) but also can be quite expensive. The result is the corporate tradition of paying a monthly commutation allowance to employees of anything up to ¥50,000 ($500) based on the duration of the daily journey.

This is obviously an opportunity for a little extra pocket money and it's not uncommon for someone to use a parent's address further away from the office and claim a higher allowance than the one for where they actually live.

The advantage of the commutation allowance to the employee is that it is non-taxable whereas a living allowance (rent support) would be. This does though mean that employees are incentivized to live further away from an office to avoid the high rents in-city and incur greater commutes than would otherwise be the case. The two hour commute is not going anywhere fast.

As a commutation allowance is typically associated with a local payroll it is usually not applicable to expatriates. I once worked with an expat who became very upset that his Japanese colleagues received this allowance to which he himself wasn't entitled. I offered to exchange it for his housing, home-leave and club membership allowances but he decided that some things were better left undisturbed and quietly shut up after that.

When is a bonus not a bonus? – when it's a loan

Post-war, capital, as with everything else, was in very limited supply. As a result, Japanese industry created an approach to borrowing from employees at interest free rates. The approach to this was to introduce a bonus system, which at first sight appears counter intuitive.

The process was to take the annual salary and divide it by seventeen. Workers would then be paid one seventeenth of their annual salary each month and three seventeenths in summer and the remaining four seventeenths in winter.

The total income remained the same however the workers were effectively providing an interest free loan to the employers. Remarkably the employee was also happy as they perceived they were receiving two guaranteed bonuses each year. Go figure, as it were.

This had two long-term effects. The first was that workers came to expect their annual bonus rather than see it as some form of conditional reward. It was, in effect, a repayment of a loan and therefore there became no association of performance related pay around this.

This remains the situation in many companies today, especially the older industries. Brands entering the

Japanese market tend to adopt more performance related rewards however this still needs to be clearly explained when hiring employees as, especially for those of the older generation, they may still expect that the bonus is guaranteed.

The second effect was that loans and hire purchase agreements also became structured around it. If you bought a car, the financing company would approach your own company's HR department to confirm what the bonus payments will be.

As a result, employees can be concerned when entering a company that doesn't pay fixed bonuses as this may cause difficulties with financing arrangements. Even though they are actually receiving the same amount on an annual basis and in fact they are receiving it earlier.

Arriving to work in a foreign company in Japan, it may at first sight appear unusual that staff at all levels receive a bonus. This tends to be a legacy of the old system where all staff received the summer and winter balloon payments. Without it though, recruitment can become problematic as the work force essentially expects there will be some form of bonus in their remuneration irrespective of level.

Even adopting the approach of increasing base salary to compensate for elimination of a bonus structure for lower level employees may be counter productive. New recruits will still expect the bonus and will not see the increase in base salary being implemented. Altering this will effectively increase the companies fixed costs as the base salary will necessarily rise to incentivize new recruits to join.

It may, in certain cases, be financially beneficial to the company to continue with the bonus structure and the new employees will be less concerned even though the perception of their remuneration package is actually costing them real yen.

Over the last decade this position has slowly been changing. The concept of a target based bonus is beginning to be understood and, if somewhat sporadically, becoming accepted. However, the large industrial behemoths will still retain the old approach whereby 90% of the payment is essentially guaranteed and the remainder is a matter for negotiation between the unions and the management. One side will eventually claim victory but the difference will have been, to all intents and purposes, a moral rather than financial trophy.

However, especially in the foreign brands entering the Japanese market, a competence basis whereby targets are established and achieved or not, the results of which directly affect the scale of the annual payout, is beginning to be more accepted. Performance based bonuses are here.

Over a decade ago, the company I was working in decided to abandon the traditional bonus in favor of a performance one. We spent months explaining to all employees the implications, their base salaries were reset and targets were established, agreed and signed off.

At the end of the first year I can still remember the sales team walking into the president's office one by one. I can also remember half of them coming out in tears when they learned that by missing their targets they had also missed their bonus. They simply hadn't believed, or comprehended, that by moving to a performance based remuneration package, they were going to be measured on performance. They simply hadn't understood the concept.

The coda to this is that come the second year of the new approach, every single salesman met or exceeded his (there were only men in the sales team in those days) targets. And those who had materially exceeded their targets, were materially rewarded. Performance can be a hard task-master, but it does work.

Data Privacy – applicable to all but you

In the mid-2000s, Japan enacted strict data privacy laws applicable to all personal data collected by companies, agencies and government organizations. There are quite severe penalties for those breaching these laws and in the case of a corporate entity there is the risk of significant reputational risk as well.

If a corporate entity accidentally releases personal data, whether through weakness of internal controls or through unforeseen circumstance, they may be required to report the loss to the appropriate authority. It may also be necessary to take out a newspaper advertisement notifying the general public of the loss. In effect this is a notification that the brand didn't take it's responsibilities seriously, no matter how unreasonable this may be.

For example, the company will still be liable if an employee at a third party Customer Service Center accesses consumer data and uses this to contact the individual. The company has little or no way to control this but is still held to be responsible. As you might guess, I've actually seen this one happen. If you have concerns over data privacy, bring your legal team in as soon as possible.

However, and for whatever reason, no one seems too concerned when this relates to yourself. For many years I would make a regular transfer from my overseas bank to my Japanese one for living expenses. I was therefore somewhat surprised when I received a call from my Japanese bank to confirm the nature of this payment and to authorize it for my account.

I of course said yes and then asked why they were asking, as I'd never received this call before despite many years of making the same regular transfer. The bank politely apologized and explained that the person in my company who normally approved the transfer had left and so they needed to call me directly.

It has to be said I was floored by this. This was a private transfer from one personal account to another personal account. But then again, all I wanted was the cash in my account and the person had only been trying to help. Time to let that one go.

Dress Code – what exactly is "Cool Biz"

Japan remains predominantly conservative in dress code. Suit and tie remain the norm in the office and despite many companies moving to casual dress, there remains a core of people uncomfortable not only with dressing casually in the office but also to be seen dressed casually on the way to work.

There still remain examples, especially amongst the older generation, of people suiting up to leave the house and changing into casual gear after arriving at the office. In many cases this is due to their spouse thinking they have actually been fired if they leave the house in anything other than a suit.

This began to change in 2005 when the then Prime Minister, Junichiro Koizumi, announced the *Cool Biz* campaign. In Japan the highest power demand comes not in winter to warm homes and offices but during summer to cool them. Air-conditioning is a huge power drain.

The idea behind Cool Biz was to encourage everyone to increase the temperature on their air-conditioning systems by one degree from 27°C to 28°C and remove their ties to keep cool. The idea slowly caught on and it became more and more acceptable to go without a tie, especially in the summer months. It should also be noted it saved millions of tons of carbon emissions each year as well.

The practice really exploded in 2011 following the Tohoku earthquake. The loss of Fukushima and the shutdown of almost the entire nuclear generating capacity across Japan led to exceptional measures. The lack of a necktie almost became a badge of honor as people worked to reduce their power consumption.

Cool Biz and the lack of a necktie are now widely accepted in the Japanese work environment however this relates largely to the internal dealings of a company. When visiting other companies, whether they are clients or suppliers, the formal suit with tie remains the standard approach. Sometimes this is actually turned to an advantage and in a meeting someone might suggest everyone go "Cool Biz" and the ties will come off to smiles all around.

If your company is a casual one, when visiting a business partner a suit with or without tie is fine as is jacket and trousers. A polo shirt is not a good idea, especially on the first introductions. The creative guys can get away with it, the rest just look like they slept rough the night before.

Clubs and cards – remember it's her job!

If an old Japan hand asks you for a few business cards it means he's planning a night out. In the clubs and hostess bars it would be rude to refuse to present a business card if asked and look incompetent if you had to say you didn't have any. Best to provide a card and make sure it's someone else's.

And then of course, you can hear whether they actually did call or not, plus you won't have those decorative invitation cards arriving every month which inevitably get left face up on your desk to the amusement of everyone around. Don't get me wrong, I'm not advocating identity theft here, just letting you know what the person asking for your cards is planning.

In my previous book "The Beginner's Guide to Japan" I talk about the pitfalls and misconceptions surrounding Hostess Clubs. In summary, they are expensive, almost exclusively Japanese speaking and the lady remains seated at the end of the evening.

Most clubs are perfectly reputable with the lady essentially performing the same task as a barmaid in western countries (she laughs at your jokes, fills your drink and helps you relax after a long day). The one difference is that an element of her job is to persuade customers to return and to do this she will most likely text or phone a client that has provided their own business card.

This can lead to an element of embarrassment for the newcomer when their assistant puts through a call from a very nice lady called Crystal who you apparently met the evening before. Your assistant will then fall off her chair laughing. As will everyone else when she tells them.

Is he sleeping or thinking? – could be either

It is not an uncommon experience to witness the sleeping salaryman in a meeting. Is he asleep or is he just resting his eyes and thinking? In reality, it's more than likely that someone is actually sleeping and over the years I've seen this remedied with an array of solutions from a gentle nudge to the outright use of a water pistol wielded by a French maid! Somewhere in between is probably appropriate.

Within domestic companies this is acceptable and is generally overlooked. However, in a foreign company, the person has chosen to work in an international environment and should comply with the norms of foreign business etiquette. Sleeping is not a good statement to the boss.

There is though, at least one instance when sleeping is understandable. If a company goes to an off-site meeting, the event is only tax deductible if there has actually been some form of formal discussion or presentation. It's not uncommon for companies to organize a seemingly irrelevant presentation, knowing that most of the attendees will sleep through it in anticipation of the party that is going to be held in the evening.

Madogiwazoku – moving closer to extinction

The *madogiwazoku* is the "man who sits by the window reading a magazine". For whatever reason he is no longer of value or use to a company but is close to retirement and just sitting out his time until he can collect his benefit in full.

Although somewhat thinned out during the financial crisis following the Lehman shock, this individual is still not quite extinct. The recession has ushered in a distinct change in Japan and redundancy and lay-offs are no longer the taboo subjects they were once. Economic reality is catching up with everyone. Even for the man by the window.

Sometimes you're just not going to understand

In the late 1980s as the asset bubble in Japan was approaching its peak, there was a women in Osaka who acted as a financial advisor and was actually very successful and well known in the city. Many rich and famous people were coming to her for advice.

The only issue was that she wasn't a professional advisor with a background in the latest financial techniques but the owner of a quiet bar in the center of town and she took her instructions from a large stone toad approximately four feet high.

When the bubble collapsed in the 1990s she was hauled out as a fraud and a charlatan. The fact that she would ask the toad for advice directly in front of the client was quietly forgotten and she was eventually prosecuted receiving quite a severe jail sentence.

This was around the time I first arrived in Japan and I asked one of my managers why people had gone along with the advice especially knowing the woman had no knowledge of finance and that she was receiving her tips from, of all things, a large stone amphibian. He looked at me and explained that what I didn't understand was that the woman herself was very persuasive and the toad had a good track record in these areas.

Sometimes you know when to stop asking. However, you quickly learn that unless you ask the correct question, don't expect to get the right answer. And sometime you're just not going to understand.

How to survive Product

This section is written specifically for the expat who will be working with product, something physical that you are selling in the market in Japan. Whether it relates to footwear, cars or cans of beer there are certain elements of Japanese market practices that are materially different to working in a western environment.

At first these differences may appear driven by outdated market practices and in many cases this may well be the case. For example, merchandising as a discipline, simply didn't exist in Japan until the last one or two decades. Prior to that it was the manufacturer (or distributor in the case of a foreign brand) that would instruct a retailer what they were to buy, and if it didn't sell, they would simply take it back and recycle it somewhere else.

However, in a number of instances, the seemingly peculiar and inefficient processes are actually driven by market reality; lack of storage capacity and multi-branded retail being two of the key issues that may differ significantly from a home market.

As a result, this section is not specifically relevant to either the service sector or one under specific government regulation and so if you are in those areas feel free to skip ahead. However, you may find it interesting, though not particularly relevant, as it reflects the Japanese approach to issue resolution and provides answers to some of the everyday questions and issues faced when working with product in the market.

Kakeritsu – how does that work again?

Apart from in a very limited number of cases, the traditional western "list price" model doesn't apply in Japan. The familiar process of establishing a fixed price for an item and then offering discounts for various benefits such as volume, payment terms, on time receipt etc remains rare, if not almost non-existent. In its place is the Japanese *kakeritsu* model.

The kakeritsu is the ratio of the wholesale price to the recommended retail price. Simply put, if an item retails for 100 and wholesales for 55, then the kakeritsu is 55%. The key difference to understanding kakeritsu is that it is negotiated on a seasonal basis and it is the percentage that is the point of discussion rather than the price.

The second difference is that the kakeritsu will typically be set by *account* rather than by *product* which leads to the effect that the same product may be being sold to two separate accounts under identical terms in relation to volume, delivery and payment terms but at different prices.

In addition to this, many brands will also offer a more attractive kakeritsu on a particular range of product for promotional purposes however again this is usually applicable to an entire range rather than a specific product.

This system, at first sight, may seem inefficient from the perspective of both parties. The negotiated price is somewhat haphazard and more a measure of the skill of the salesman than a reflection of the commercial value of a product. Added to this the account has minimum incentive, once the kakeritsu has been established, to improve the sales growth in-season.

Moving to "trade terms" where prices are fixed and the discounts are based effectively on performance would seem more beneficial to all parties. From the brand's perspective there is a direct incentive for the account to improve performance and from the account's perspective, they gain control of their own margin.

The picture, as always, is not quite as straightforward as this though. In reality, the sales team and the account will work together throughout a season to continually adjust the kakeritsu such that the account's margin is effectively protected.

Although the initial go-in kakeritsu may have been 60, it may well have been reduced to 40 by the end of the season by agreement between the sales team and the account and the blended kakeritsu could be, for example, 50.

This continuous process of adjustment is effectively invisible in a large business as it may be occurring at a very detailed level. The sales teams will not only be looking to ensure the profitability of the account but also to provide additional incentives in the instance of slow moving inventory.

Without a detailed and disciplined review of the kakeritsu and margin on a regular basis, it is relatively straightforward for the new foreign manager to miss this. The forecast margin will have blended not only the kakeritsu but the expected level of markdown (rebate) provided to the account and therefore the decline will not be easily visible.

The solution to controlling this is obviously to implement strict internal controls however this can become arduous to say the least. The need to manage kakeritsu, markdowns as well as returns ensures a significant number of transactions may need to be reviewed on a weekly or even daily basis. Another reason to move to Trade Terms, where the rules are objective rather than subjective.

Trade Terms – a question of will power

Given the disproportionate benefit to the retailer of the kakeritsu model over trade terms (a list price with known and defined incentives), the account has little incentive to transition to an approach whereby they are constrained by fixed rules as they already essentially have the best of all worlds under the existing system.

Again from this perspective, for the brands it may appear that there is an unfair apportionment of risk and that the account should agree to a change of process.

The issue then becomes one of the brand trying to persuade the account to change. However the account sees this not only as a change but also as a duplication of effort unless all the remaining brands under the retailer's portfolio convert at the same time. This is highly unlikely to happen as these brands would need to persuade all their own accounts to convert as well. The entire process is fully integrated but, more to the point, fully inter-locked. Change one and you have to change them all.

A number of companies have attempted to implement this change with differing levels of success however each has had one thing in common. Scale, and with it, dominance in their market sector.

It is different if you command 25% of an accounts business than if you are a few percent. The brands that have implemented trade terms successfully were in a position to explain to the account that this is what was going to happen and not have to enter into a negotiation with them.

For a company or brand embarking on the route to conversion to trade terms, a number of reasons will be presented as to why this is not possible.

1) it's not standard market practice and therefore the accounts will neither understand nor accept the change;

2) the account's IT systems will not be able to function with two separate trading logics and

therefore, unless all accounts can be persuaded to convert, this won't be possible;

3) the company's own IT systems will be unable to function with two trading logics and therefore, if any account refuses to change, it will not be possible;

4) an account may complain to The Fair Trade Commission and an investigation may lead to sanction for the brand;

5) in changing to a fixed price list, the effective price the accounts will pay may increase and therefore not be acceptable.

All the points above have merit to one degree or another. However, the conversion from the tradition kakeritsu system to a list price is becoming in effect an operational necessity. This is due to greater and greater integration of global systems and therefore global business practices. Added to this is the commercial requirement of the brands themselves. Changing to trade terms is less of a technical issue and more of a test of the willpower and leadership.

In terms of addressing the objections that will be raised, each has prima facie merit but dig a little deeper and they begin to crumble.

Firstly it is very true that the accounts may not understand and therefore will not accept the change however, this is a question of communication and explanation. It is the role of the sales teams to communicate with accounts and they must first gain a thorough understanding of the implications themselves.

Saying that the accounts will not accept the change is more likely to be a reflection of the sales team's understanding, and to an extent, fear of the dark, more than anything else. As with all processes of change management, training and education is vital. The proper materials, both for internal and external consumption, are a critical requirement.

The sales teams can't be expected to sell a new process and concept to an account unless they fully understand and buy into it first. There may indeed be greater internal resistance to such a change than will ultimately be received from the market itself.

The second and third points are essentially *technical excuses*. Any systems change can be a significant undertaking. Each one requires detailed and time consuming planning and development by what are often limited resources. However, this is again a question of willpower rather than one of IT systems.

If the brand leadership is committed, these objections can be overcome. Although an account may insist their systems cannot be changed there is a very simple solution to this. If an account insists on a kakeritsu, then give it to them. Implementing trade terms is a conversion of principles rather than an exercise in math and IT.

The key point is that the price is no longer negotiable but established by rules. This can be calculated outside the accounts system as easily as within it. Agree the terms of trade, calculate the equivalent kakeritsu, and that's the number. The systems points are no longer an issue. Willpower is.

The fourth point regarding The Fair Trade Commission is valid though a little disingenuous. The FTC will only become involved if the brand has walked in like a bull in a china shop. Taking all reasonable steps to explain and communicate the change to an account is an obvious element of the entire process.

Any concerns can be further mitigated by adopting a phased process where the account is given one to two years notice period up front. No one said this was going to be quick and given any major IT project, a 24-month time line is not unreasonable.

The final point is perhaps the most unpalatable. When accounts have all been receiving different prices for the same product and a new, fixed price is introduced, someone is going to pay more and someone is going to pay less.

The starting point for this is the commercial strategy of the brand itself. It may opt for the change to remain neutral to its own P/L. The winners and losers effectively balance out and the brand's margin remains unchanged.

There are also the extremes whereby the decision could be there are no winners, thus maximizing the brand's returns or, alternatively, it could be that there may be no losers and the entire cost of conversion is borne by the brand itself. The answer is completely within control of the brand's management. Once the decision has been taken it is simply a matter of math to calculate which accounts receive which share of the pie.

Obviously consistency becomes important. Once the decision has been taken and the communication process started, this will be critical issue and late changes may undermine the entire project.

Capitulating to pressure from the accounts would be a sign of ultimate project failure. Some accounts were going to win and some were going to lose. This was known at the beginning and comes as no surprise, time to stand the ground.

As of the time of writing, trade terms have been implemented in one form or another by a relatively limited number of foreign brands, but they have been implemented and that's the point. It's a question of strategy and willpower and not one of immovable market practices.

The Daily Call-Off – I know, but there's a reason

For those who have arrived in Japan to work in Operations or Supply Chain, the impression of overall inefficiency can be striking. A distribution center will seem massively overstaffed, shipments and order handling still extremely manual and the cost eye-watering. That is until you dive under the surface.

The key driver of complexity of retail logistics in Japan arises from the lack of large scale storage at the retailer. Stores are more likely to be serviced directly by the distributor than through a retailer's own distribution centers, which remain few and far between.

Retailers simply do not have on or off-site storage to maintain more than a limited supply of a few days stock at most. As a result, push inventory back up the supply chain to the distributor, calling off product as needed, sometimes on a single unit basis.

This is known as the *daily call-off* and where as a retailer in another country might receive a single bulk order each month, a retailer in Japan will receive hundreds if not thousands of deliveries across their networks in a similar period.

The second issue that complicates the position is that Japan is a multi-branded retail market. The retailer has a choice which brands to purchase and stock. In a mono-branded market, such as China, the retailer effectively must do whatever is required by the distributor. In Japan they have the opportunity to simply switch orders to alternative brands (and do). The distributor has a lower ability to drive efficiency into the retailer in effect. The one who insists on bulk shipments may very soon find they've solved the delivery issue by eliminating deliveries all together.

As an example, consider the interactions between a Japanese distributor and retailer. The retailer will have placed a seasonal forecast several months prior to a season. When the time comes, the *retailer* and not the distributor, initiates the delivery instruction.

This is obviously the reverse of the western process where the distributor will ship product at the agreed time and notify the retailer. In this instance though, there is an understanding the retailer will have warehouse space sufficient to accept the shipment.

In Japan, it is less common for retailers to hold independent warehouse space and the distributor becomes the de facto storage center until the product is required.

The daily call off is thus driven by a reality of space utilization in Japan and the nature of multi-branded retail, rather than through inefficiencies in the distributor's supply chain. There are always opportunities for efficiency and these should be executed wherever possible but the market is going to continue to operate within these limitations for the foreseeable future.

Getting paid – by the box

The payment process offers an interesting new set of challenges. Whereas a conventional western process would see the seller issuing an invoice to the buyer, the buyer checking the invoice and then remitting to the seller the invoiced amount, the process is reversed in Japan.

When the product is shipped, each individual delivery will have a shipping notice attached to the outside of the carton. This note (or *dempyo*) carries both the content details as well as the pricing information (either as a kakeritsu or actual unit price).

On receipt the retailer will collect all the shipping notices, collate them after confirming accuracy, and then at the end of the month pay the distributor based on this. The retailer also sends a statement of items paid and it is then the responsibility of the distributor to reconcile shipments made to payments received *at a carton level*.

Note the reversal of the workloads. In the western approach it is the responsibility of the retailer (payer) to confirm accuracy prior to payment where as in the Japanese system it is the responsibility of the distributor (payee) to confirm completeness and accuracy.

The workload is obviously followed by the headcount. In western countries the retailer has the higher headcount in the payments department and in Japan the distributor has greater employment in the accounts receivable team.

A payment statement from a large account may run to several hundred pages each month with fifty line items on each page and at first sight it would appear that this process is crying out for automation. The difficulty again becomes one of standardization. A retailer may insist the distributor comply with their standards. The argument being that it would not be possible for the retailer to comply with the standards of a single distributor over all others. Where as the distributor has precisely the opposite problem.

Until a Japan wide standard is implemented, this will remain an issue. It even goes to the extent that each retailer requires a different format of delivery note from the distributor. Very soon, the distribution center is managing several hundred different formats of delivery note and shipping the same product to different retailers at different prices. However, despite these inherent inefficiencies I'm always impressed Japan has still built a $3 trillion economy.

Jumping tegatta – something's badly wrong

Tegatta are more commonly known as p-notes, short for "promissory note". They are still the standard form of corporate payment in Japan today. It is essentially a post-dated cheque used by companies to defer payment for 90 or 120 days. The period is a matter of negotiation between the two parties so can be anything from 30 to 180 days in some instances.

The difference between a p-note and a cheque is that the p-note is more like a non-cancelable bearer bond that can be presented for payment without proof of ownership or identity. The instrument grew out of the post-war need for credit and liquidity in the market and effectively extended the corporate sectors credit by several months.

The notes do expire but not for several months after the presentation date. This means, if you lose one, you have a serious problem. They tend to be used only for high value payments, such as inventory and so the value can often be for millions of dollars.

Many years ago I heard a story of a colleague at a different company who actually once did lose a p-note for slightly over $1million. They never did work out where it went but think it got caught up when they were clearing up the department in advance of a visit from head office (there's an irony if ever there was one).

It was fourteen months before they could ask the company to issue a new note as there was no way to cancel the old one. The company, understandably, didn't want two notes for the same amount floating in the market. Fourteen months of hoping it had been destroyed in the clear out and that no one else would present it to the bank!

The characteristic of the notes has two interesting properties. Firstly, if a note is not honored within two weeks of its presentation date, you have the right to place the offending company into liquidation to recover your funds. In reality this almost never happens. A company, aware that it is in financial difficulty, will approach its creditors first and request that they do not actually present the notes for clearing.

This is called *jumping tegatta* and a sure sign that a company is close to bankruptcy. In over twenty years in Japan, of all the companies that have approached me and asked that I defer presentation of their p-notes, not a single one is still in business today. If ever asked to do this, start recovering your funds as quickly as possible and convert terms to cash on delivery.

Inventory Management – it's not rocket science

Inventory management has never truly been an interesting topic of conversation it has to be said. In Japan, where interest rates have been effectively zero since the early 1990s, the holding cost of inventory has not been a subject for discussion or debate until very recently. The recent economic crisis has meant companies have started to look at not only their P&Ls but also their balance sheets. And many have been a little shocked with what they've found.

I once received a call from the global CFO of the company I was working for at the time. He asked me how the inventory levels were and I replied "no problem at all, we have loads of it". His response was "that's the point".

More companies go bankrupt because they run out of cash than ones that are actually loss making. His point to me was that we were using our cash flow to finance unnecessary inventory, and worse, we were doing this because we simply weren't looking at it. And he was right.

Inventory management isn't rocket science. It's simply discipline. Bring the product in just before you need it, and when it's not selling, clear it as fast as you can because things are not going to get much better. It sounds simple but due to the low marginal cost of borrowing it has been a somewhat neglected management skill in Japan. Indeed, the finance team is probably not even looking at the subject in most cases unless forced to by their foreign head office.

Forecasting inventory is actually relatively simple. Take a spreadsheet and map out forecast monthly sales for the next twelve months. Next, look at the forecast margin for these sales and use that to calculate the inventory being sold.

The next line is to look at inbound forecasts and subtracting one from the other gives you the net movement in inventory, on a monthly basis, over the period. Add in your starting position and you have your inventory level, neatly laid out over a twelve-month period. From this it becomes a simple matter of how to calculate the inventory turn. Choose a definition of this and stick to it. Each is as good as the next but seven or thirteen month trailing averages are the common ones.

The advantage of using the thirteen month trailing average is that it shows a more holistic view of the inventory position over a full annual cycle. The disadvantage is that it takes a significant period to influence the indicator. Over a period of months it can become demoralizing to not see any results from the work and effort. The results are there, it's simply a question of time to see the effects.

The advantages and disadvantages of using the seven-month average are the reverse of this. The effects appear relative quickly however it is less representative of a cyclical business.

The discipline comes in by ensuring the right people are all in a review meeting at the right time. The meeting should be based around the update cycle of sales forecasts which means, in effect, probably monthly. The attendance should include not just the finance team but all stake holders. This means the supply chain, sales, retail and eCom teams as well as the product marketing and brand marketing teams. Almost everyone becomes a stakeholder when the entire inventory chain is reviewed.

Very quickly you'll find that this becomes a genuine cross-functional team and people want to attend as it becomes a de facto monthly business review.

If you're a product based business and your inventory turn is below two, you need to spend more time on inventory management. If you claim your inventory turn is over ten, you need to check your numbers, given daily shipment, slow moving stock and inbound customs controls, someone is being creative with the math.

Each business category will have different best in class inventory turn levels but by focusing on the subject, a company can always improve where it is. Managing inventory levels means not just ensuring you have the right inventory at the right time but also that you avoid both stock outs and excessive holding costs.

In the first two years of improved management, we saved over $5 million in the example I referenced above. And watch out for the January, February inbound numbers. Everyone targets the year-end but all the good work can be thrown away if the first few months of the year are not managed well.

Inventory clearance is actually relatively straightforward in Japan. Destroying the product is tax deductible as long as you can clearly document this happening and photographs are useful evidence for this.

However, Japan has an outstanding Factory Outlet footprint. Here Factory Outlet malls are a family day out. They are high quality, friendly and reasonably accessible. The entire family will spend a day strolling around, walking the dog and having lunch. And also buying as much product as they can carry.

The outlet malls are designed as premium retail space. Brands that use them effectively provide a brand story and an introduction to the full price product retailed in-city. Rather than being brand negative, the Factory Outlet allows a brand to manage inventory clearance in a way that will actually be positive to its overall story.

A number of brands actually develop product for Factory Outlet. They no longer clear excess inventory in this way but run the outlets as a business in their own right.

So, inventory management is relatively straight forward, you just need to be on top of it, involve all the right players, make decisions in real time and consider Factory Outlet as an opportunity rather than a threat. And suddenly inventory management is no longer a dull and boring subject but a completely new business opportunity.

Channels and the FTC – they enjoy a good visit

When the FTC (Fair Trade Commission) is annoyed they tend to let you know in quite a spectacular fashion. Raids are rare in Japan but when they happen the TV stations will all have been notified in advance and the suits will turn out in force. And if you're a foreign company, there's not much downside for them to be seen to be heavy handed.

Computers will be either seized or hard drives copied, files will be collected into cardboard boxes and hauled out of the building and the "interviews" will last weeks if not months.

The raids will also be simultaneously organized across the country if there are multiple locations of interest. Whilst walking into the Tokyo office, the Osaka and Nagoya branches will receive a visit at the same time. Potentially so will multiple business partners. You're not going to keep this quiet and on the evening news your company logo is probably going to feature quite highly.

FTC investigations are almost always as a result of a specific complaint rather than any form of on-going activities. Foreign brands in Japan this can be used as a direct tactic by the competition to tie them up in red tape for months.

The complaint itself may be about something minor that a company has done or it may actually reflect the fact that it has annoyed the counter-party in some way and now it's payback time. You also have no right to know the counterparty. You never get to face your accuser in court.

The usual trigger for an FTC investigation relates to price controls. On the face of it Japan is seen as a country with vast administration controlling almost everything but in reality it is actual less so than its reputation would suggest. Writing to an account and telling they can no longer receive product because they are discounting is a sure fire way to trigger an investigation. Similarly, withholding shipments for reasons other than the retailer is no longer brand appropriate or bankrupt will be deemed a transgression. Anything to do with price control is a taboo subject.

The reason that the FTC tend to take such a high profile approach to investigations though is that the actual punishments may be quite light. Effectively they are attempting to embarrass the brand into compliance. A company that is found to be a first time offender may simply receive a written warning. This will escalate for further offences but is highly unlikely to reach the ultimate level of a custodial sentence for the Representative Director. Sentences for white-collar crime in Japan remain relatively lenient unless, of course, you upset the establishment, and then you're going to jail.

This raises the obvious question as to whether it is possible to control brand distribution in the market place at all. Clearly channel segmentation is important for a brand and appearing in the correct channels is not only a question of brand image but one of reaching the appropriate consumer.

Although adopting an approach of price control to avoid the discount channels is clearly against the remit of the FTC, ensuring that your product appears in "brand appropriate" locations is perfectly legitimate. It is important to be able to clearly answer the question as to what defines a brand appropriate channel but once this has been addressed the FTC is at least open to the argument that there are right and wrong distribution patterns for a product.

If it can clearly be demonstrated that a channel is brand inappropriate and therefore detrimental to the overall business then it may be accepted that business can be controlled directly in the market place. Therefore, if terminating or refusing access to product, it is necessary to focus purely on the arguments as to whether the brand should be appearing at those particular distribution points at all. The question of price maintenance should not be a consideration. To ensure no significant questions arise from the FTC, it should simply not be discussed in any format.

An Expat in Japan

Being an effective expat in Japan comes with the same principles and guidelines of being an effective manager in any country. Having understood some of the basic elements of the corporate landscape, the next step is to consider how to actually apply these.

The following section examines a number of differences between Western and Japanese business styles and will identify some of the more subtle points that are important but easily overlooked. If nothing else, the most valuable lesson of this section to take away is, *if you think you understand what is happening, take another look.*

So what exactly goes into an expat package?

The typical expat package is designed to provide a reasonable standard of living and compensation for transferring away from a home country. The head office will usually complain that expats are too expensive. However, when asked, I have seen people literally recoil in horror at the suggestion that they might transfer themselves. Expats are more expensive than local hire but they are bringing a skill set unavailable in the local market. The compensation is designed to reflect the impacts on life and lifestyle.

The irony here is that many companies will have a policy that once an expat has been in a country for a certain period of time they must transfer to a domestic package or leave for a new posting.

The effect of this is that once an expat has become really effective in a market after maybe three, four or five years they have a choice. To accept a significantly reduced standard of living or be replaced by someone who has none of the skills and experience developed over those years.

The additional costs incurred in supporting an expat are real and can easily be a multiple of the price a local hire. Over the years there has been a regular pendulum swing on this issue in Japan. A company, previously managed by a foreigner, brings in a local hire to save cost. Things don't work out, usually due to communication or cultural issues and so the company switches back to the expat. And so the cycle begins again.

The packages obviously differ company to company and grade to grade but in general fall into two distinct groups. The first is an onshore domestic contract with additional benefits becoming an employee of the local company for the duration of the secondment. The second is an offshore package where the contract is held through a third country, often Hong Kong for expats based in Japan. This will include tax protection as well as additional benefits to make the position attractive to the expat.

Whether the contract should be onshore or offshore is discussed elsewhere however the benefits themselves will most likely be similar. One point though is that, with an onshore package, the expat gains all the rights and support of a normal employee. Including the difficulty in removing them if things go south. An offshore contract can include any terms and conditions the two parties agree to so in general benefits the company as much as the expat.

The elements included in a package are normally designed to ensure that the quality of life for the expat and their family remains consistent with their home country. Consistent, but not necessarily identical. Rolling grasslands are a rare sight in central Tokyo.

It would generally include a base salary that includes a cost of living adjustment and/or a quality of life adjustment, and internationalized bonus structure, housing, schooling for children, medical insurance, retirement contributions, home leave for the family, adjusted vacation allowances and possibly club membership.

If an employment contract is *onshore* there is only one structure. This is effectively a regular employment contract with the local company and in addition includes any separately agreed extras. The expat is paid net of taxes which are deducted by the company in the regular payroll.

If the contract is *offshore*, there are two basic structures to it though anything can be included in this structure provided it complies with the seconding country's laws and regulations. The contract can either be gross or net of tax.

In the instance of a contract that is gross of tax, it is assumed that the expat will be liable for all tax exposure in Japan and the contract payment will be grossed up to reflect this. If it is paid net of tax, the company assumes the tax liability and the expat is paid a lower amount monthly but has no exposure to tax or changes in tax law.

The usual format is to use a net contract as this brings security to the expat and a possible saving to the company dependent on a number of issues. A gross contract provides certainty to the company but leaves a significant exposure to the expat who must ensure they conserve funds throughout the year to pay the tax when it becomes due. Unless they know what they're doing this can be quite problematic and so contracts tend not to be structured this way.

Whether onshore or offshore, in March each year the expat then makes a tax filing for the benefits in kind (housing, schooling etc). The liability for these addition benefits will be defined in the original transfer agreement. The difference may be material depending on whether the individual is a Board director of the company. This is usually the case for a president position but not necessarily for others.

A *housing allowance* should come as standard. These vary depending on city, grade and whether the expat is married and also whether there are children. In Tokyo a typical allowance for an unmarried senior manager level would be ~¥600,000 ($6,000) per month and increase to ~¥1.5m ($15,000) for a president, married with children.

These may sound high numbers but are certainly not the top of the market. This accolade typically goes for the financial industries and these can be significantly more. It is also becoming more common that companies will offer incentives to reduce these amounts. In some cases if the expat chooses to live at a lower cost the company will split the saving with them.

One final point on housing is that it is becoming more common for companies to agree to allow the expat to use the housing allowance as mortgage support. This effectively allows the purchase of their own property. This is very beneficial for the experienced expat who will be stable in a new environment but are uncommon for first timers where the situation can be more volatile until they settle.

In Tokyo, where the residential housing, market is 80% down on it's 1990's peaks, this is a very attractive proposition as it would be hard to lose. The company will often require there be no additional expense. As a result an allowance structured as mortgage support will be lower than a conventional housing allowance as the tax rates are significantly different.

Home-leave is an important element of the package especially in the instance of a married expat with family. When you live overseas it becomes normal to travel to the home country once or twice a year simply to keep in contact with family and also to manage stress levels.

Some companies allow the expat to travel anywhere instead of the home country to recharge their batteries. Others require it to be to the home country itself. Again there is a difference in tax treatment between home country and third country so this should be clarified before signing.

Schooling is also important. International schools charge annual fees in the region of ~¥2.5m ($25,000) plus enrolment fees. A family of three, with tax included is therefore going to cost in the region of $120,000 in education fees alone each year. This is one to be very clear on in the original contract as the option to send children to a local Japanese school is possible but not very optimal for the kids themselves especially if the assignment is only two or three years. Going home may well be more difficult for them than arriving in the first place with the slow language development and very different learning styles and syllabus. Local schools are Japanese language only, there will be no English either in class or in the playground.

The *vacation allowance* should take account of the differences between the standard in the home and local country. In Germany, for example, five weeks vacation is relatively normal whereas in Japan two or three weeks are standard. It can come as a shock when you find you actually don't have enough leave to use the home leave budget you were so careful to negotiate.

Club membership is really down to the company policy. The Tokyo American Club is the most common in Tokyo as it provides good facilities and an instant network for newcomers. There are others but membership tends to be on a case-by-case basis.

One element that is rarely included in an expat package in Japan but very common elsewhere in Asia is the question of a live-in maid. Although maids are relatively common amongst the expat community, the additional cost of living quarters tends to make the option of supporting one in-house quite rare though not unheard of.

If you sponsor a maid she is essentially tied to your requirements though free to use her own time as she wishes. The company will often assist in this sponsorship program but after that, the living arrangements are down to the individual.

The advantages of the offshore contract

As mentioned there are many forms of contract an expatriate can work under in Japan. The offshore contract is where the individual is technically employed by a group company outside Japan and then seconded to the one in Japan.

Both versions are valid for visa purposes and, assuming there is no intention to evade income tax, both are perfectly legal. The offshore contract though has two significant advantages for the non-Japanese expatriate.

The first advantage relates to taxable income. In the first five years of residence in Japan, the taxable liability of an expatriate is determined based on the higher of the *time-apportioned income* and the *salary remitted into Japan*.

Therefore, if an expatriate is employed overseas and is paid overseas, they can significantly reduce their taxable liability. For example, if a person travels 25% of their time but only remits 50% of their salary into Japan, then they are liable for tax on only 75% of their income. If they were paid 100% directly into Japan, as would be the case on a local contract, then the liability would be on 100% of income.

This can become a significant saving over time. As marginal rates are currently 50%, this provides a valuable opportunity for the expatriate to legally reduce their tax exposure but only applies in the first five years of residency, after that, tax is assessed on worldwide income and the benefit disappears.

The second advantage of an offshore contract is that there is no liability for social insurance. Social insurance is currently close to 20%, paid equally by the company and the employee. As the liability attaches to the company, if an expatriate is employed locally, there is no option but to pay up.

However, Japanese social security obviously doesn't attach to a non-Japanese entity and therefore by contracting to an offshore entity and being seconded to Japan, both the company and the expatriate can benefit from this arrangement.

The implications of not contributing to social insurance are that the expatriate loses their right to a Japanese pension on retirement and the 70% discount on Japanese medical fees. Neither of these are likely to be significant issues as the company will, more likely than not, have a corporate pension in place as well as private medical insurance. Always worth checking with a tax accountant but at the time of writing this is legal and very beneficial to both company and individual.

The Business Meeting – more than meets the eye

The first thing you will notice about a business meeting in Japan is that there are too many people in the room. If someone is coming to your company for a meeting it is generally considered polite to bring more people than necessary as a sign of commitment.

It does mean though that you regularly need a larger room or more chairs. This rule also stands in the instance you are visiting someone on business. You should not only take your translator but at least one other person who is familiar with the company or situation.

If you are the visitor, then your seat should always be on the side of the table facing the door (which typically means you will also have your back to the window), and vice versa if someone is visiting your office. As everyone enters the room, the first thing is always to exchange the all important business card with anyone you're meeting for the first time. Nothing will happen until this is complete and there will be minimal conversation until the last cards are exchanged.

Naturally there is also an appropriate order to sit around the table. This is the other reason you brought your colleague as they will be able to direct you to the correct chair. This allows the correct people to be facing each other. The position are usually arranged so as to avoid any difficulty of having to talk up and down the table.

It is very common that tea, coffee, water or some beverage is served in the meeting. This will be pre-organized and it's a good idea to simply go with the flow rather than asking for something specific as chaos may ensue. The host always invites the guests to start drinking before themselves and until offered it's unlikely they will begin.

The close of a meeting can sometimes be a drawn out affair. If you feel the meeting is over and the conversation becoming uncomfortable it's probably because everyone is waiting politely for you to bring it to an end. To do this, simply place both hands of the table, pause to let everyone see, and thank everyone for coming. This will be reciprocated and the meeting is officially over.

The Greeting and the Business Card

A *meishi* (business card) is not simply a collection of contact details but more a statement of identity; it represents who you are and your hierarchical position in relation to the person you are greeting. As such the business card is always treated with an air of respect.

A Japanese person will never write on someone's business card or put it directly into their wallet or, worse still, put it in a wallet and the sit on it. They may as well have just written on someone's face and then sat on their head.

Although it may seem a little excessive, there is a protocol to presenting and receiving a business card. It should always be presented two handed, standing facing the receiver and with due care and courtesy. At the same time you will be being offered the other person's business card, which you should accept with your right hand.

There are many stories of the need then to make a comment such as noting the person's title or confirming the address. However, I have rarely seen this and almost always by a foreigner. In reality it appears to be one of those urban myths about business in Japan. It is perfectly sufficient to thank the person and say that it is a pleasure to meet them.

One caveat is that it is generally considered a major business faux pas to offer your business card to someone twice. It is effectively saying you have forgotten them from the previous meeting. If you find yourself in the unfortunate position of doing this and notice that the atmosphere in the room has suddenly turned to one of shock, the face saving response is to say this is your new card with some updated information and you would like to give it to them for their records. Stress levels will come down and honor will have been satisfied.

One useful technique is to get into the habit of checking in advance whether the people you are meeting are new to you or not. As you may be the only foreigner in the room, it is often easier for your Japanese counterpart to remember you than for you to remember them. This isn't being impolite, it's simply a result of you standing out more than others may and you will find thcy will know more easily whether this is the first meeting or not.

One very helpful way to use the meishi you collect in a meeting is to neatly arrange them in front of you in the order the people are sitting across the table. This helps with remembering names especially in the early days when you are not only learning someone's name but also a completely new word too in most cases. If you cannot remember which card belongs to which person then still neatly arrange them in front of you but this time in order of seniority. It will be noticed and both your own team and the people you are meeting will appreciate your actions.

The Aisatsu – the important art of doing nothing

The *aisatsu* is a special and rather peculiar form of initial business meeting. If someone is new to Japan and senior in the company then the chances are they are going to be having a number of these in the very near future.

An aisatsu is purely an introductory meeting arranged so that a new business partners. Initially an aisatsu may appear an unproductive use of time. However in the sense of business etiquette, they are valuable and a little time invested at the beginning of a relationship can prove extremely productive in the long run.

No real business is discussed during an aisatsu as the key objective is the introduction itself. There is simply an exchange of cards and courtesies allowing both parties the time to put a face to a name. Generally, if there is important business to discuss this is only referred to obliquely as a suggestion of the need for a future meeting to discuss the subject. Aisatsu are a good opportunity to ask general questions such as their thoughts on the economy or how their business is overall.

Typically an aisatsu occurs at the time of change of roles such as when a new senior staff is promoted or when a new expat is assigned to Japan in a senior position. Within a business context, an aisatsu is taken seriously although they would only last twenty to thirty minutes however during this time all parties are taking the opportunity to quietly assess one another.

Especially in relation to a new foreigner in Japan, if it is a senior person who has arrived to meet you, they have probably seen many foreigners come and go over the years. This is an opportunity to demonstrate a willingness and openness to a new relationship and all it will cost is twenty minutes.

Stand by your word - forever

Your word is your bond. Literally. If something isn't intended it should remain unsaid. A Japanese decision is a significant commitment whereas a Western one may be simply a working solution to be updated at a later time. In the context of Japan, if someone says they will do something, they have little choice but to see this through to the end.

This is especially true in the instance of a negotiation where a verbal agreement is seen as a firm and final commitment. Breaking a commitment is seen not just to reflect poorly on the individual but on the entire company. Once agreed it might as a well have been signed in blood.

The making or breaking of a commitment is seen as a corner stone of developing and maintaining a good business relationship in Japan. I have seen orders worth millions of dollars be directed to a competitor simply because a prior commitment was seen to have been broken and the relationship suffered as a result.

Conversely I've seen orders worth millions of dollars be placed as a welcome gift for a new president replacing one who struggled with relationships.

Within this context it is also as important to remember what has not been agreed as much as what has. Going into a negotiation with a clear objective and walking out thinking that it has been settled is an error we are all guilty of from time to time. There is no harm in confirming at the end of a discussion what has been finalized and what remains a work in process. And this should always be confirmed with Japanese colleagues.

Nemawashi – the art of agreement

It is a brave person who brings a fresh proposal to a meeting hoping to reach a positive outcome in Japan. Meetings tend to have too many people, old subjects already agreed will be discussed and little progress seems to be made. Ironically, one of the key complaints in Japanese business brought up time and again by my Japanese colleagues is that there are too many meetings. And yet people still attend even when the subject is unrelated to their responsibilities.

To a foreigner, a Japanese business meeting can seem like a confusingly inefficient use of time and the reason for this is that they often are. Even the Japanese staff can become exasperated at the lack of purpose. However, if a point is raised that actually needs a decision to be made, it is often difficult or impossible to persuade the group to agree. Or disagree.

The issue will often simply be debated and shelved for further discussion. At this point the chances of achieving alignment are quickly slipping away. The reason for this is that no one will be willing, in a group where they are unsure of others opinions, to put their own thoughts on the table. That would be stepping out of line.

The solution to this problem, and how to ensure agreement is reached quickly is the process of *nemawashi*, "preparing the roots". If a meeting goes smoothly and a decision is confirmed quickly and easily, that's because the actual decision has been made before the meeting even starts. In fact, the meeting will have been called only after everyone is already in alignment.

For those who remember, this becomes a little like an episode of "Yes Minister". The meeting can't be held until the conclusion has been agreed. If it were held before this, they may come to the wrong conclusion.

The approach to achieving a successful outcome is to discuss the subject in advance with each of the key stakeholders individually. Hear their opinions and receive their tentative approval of the proposal before moving to a more public forum for discussion. Any key issues can be sounded out, concerns raised privately and objections addressed all in the quiet privacy of a one-on-one conversation.

The objective of nemawashi is always to ensure that the decision has been made before the meeting and the meeting itself is purely a rubber stamp. Nobody is surprised, all concerns have already been addressed and all key participants are in alignment. Achieving a decision is then a very simple process. Nemawashi, the art of getting things done.

The corporate night out – who pays again?

In western business practice, generally speaking it is standard procedure that, on a business night out, the most senior person present should pay at the end of the evening. This ensures that someone who wasn't present authorizes the expense claim and by default they will be more senior to anyone who participated in the evening.

Japan is the opposite. The account will either be settled by one of the most junior people in the group or may not even be settled at all but charged directly through to the company. It is seen as something essentially below the senior people present to become involved in such matters such as settling an account.

With the level of corporate hospitality in Japan this can become something of an issue. Although the regular expensive dinners followed by drinks in a high priced bar are significantly less common than in the past, they have been replaced by more modest priced dinners and drinks in a regular bar rather than being eliminated completely.

Regular contact with business partners and indeed colleagues and staff remain an important element of business life in Japan, one that binds the corporate world ever tighter together. As a result, it's important to establish the ground rules at the beginning.

Japanese staff present on a night out will most likely automatically assume that standard protocols apply and it's important to be clear this is not the case if you are the new senior in the company.

Footwear, and what lies beneath

Taking off your shoes is an absolute must when entering someone's home. The area around the door (the genkan) is there specifically for this and the shoes will be neatly gathered together and turned around ready for slipping on when leaving. Often a pair of slippers will be provided but it's absolutely inconceivable to walk into someone's house with shoes still on feet.

This leads to a specific, though somewhat comical, issue. Whenever leaving the house it's a good idea to ensure the socks are new and don't have holes in them. The reason for this is that it is not only customary to take shoes off when entering someone's house, it's also common in many restaurants and even some offices. And a little pinky poking out will be the cause of much hilarity!

How to pour someone's drink – and your own!

Interestingly for foreigners, beer is the usual choice of drink even at major events. Bottles will be on tables and glasses full of foam. If others are ordering wine, then it's OK to order as well but if they're ordering a beer, go with the flow, there's a reason for it.

In Japan it's considered polite to pour each other's drinks and also top them up when you see them going down. The glasses are more akin to shot glasses and the beer will be served from bottles on the table (don't order draft beer, it ruins the effect). So as the person across the table is filling your glass, it provides a regular opportunity to talk and generally be jovial.

However, that's only half the story. When you offer someone to fill their glass, etiquette dictates that they should take at least a token drink unless the glass is empty, in which case fill it to the brim.

If you think about it, this is actually a stealth approach to regulating how quickly the people around the table become intoxicated. The pourer is controlling the rate at which everyone else is drinking. And no one can be blamed as it's just being polite!

Importantly, you should never pour your own drink unless you know what your doing. It's mildly impolite (and also curses you with bad luck that you won't be getting married for the next three years, in case this is a concern). The reason to try to avoid it is it deprives the others at the table of the opportunity to pour for you. However, an empty glass rarely remains empty for long.

It's actually also a very good way of moving between tables at a corporate event to talk to different groups of people. It's perfectly acceptable to simply grab a full bottle and go over to the next table (assuming the next table is also from your company) and offer drinks. A seat will soon appear for you and everyone will invite you to sit with them and suddenly your talking with another group and hearing completely new stories.

Managing a Japanese team – the art of listening

In many ways, managing a team or company in Japan is similar to managing one in a Western environment. People respond to direction, clarity, fairness and look for inspiration and motivation. The difference comes in the execution rather than the principle.

Managing a team in Japan may vary from company to company or even from department to department. However, the common theme throughout is that it will require a new approach to ensuring objectives are aligned, implemented and ultimately achieved. As will be discussed elsewhere, receiving a "yes" does not necessarily mean everyone is in agreement. In fact it can be a very simple way to bring a discussion to an end for the sake of avoiding further discussion.

In Western business this may lead to repercussions for the individuals involved for being less than transparent. In Japan this is unlikely to be the case in this context and a more comprehensive approach may be required.

The following are a simple set of guidelines that highlight some of the differences experienced when working in Japan and how to be more effective in a new management role.

Speaking English doesn't mean understanding

It is fairly simple to assume that just because someone speaks English well automatically means that they understand to the same level. I speak Japanese well and can communicate almost anything I want to fluently. That doesn't mean that when someone replies using full speed, colloquial, native Japanese I am going to understand. It is a very simple assumption to make and the level of misunderstanding may become significant. The normal rules of communication apply with the emphasis on *speaking simply, clearly, repetitively and avoiding idioms.*

The reverse of this is to assume that if someone doesn't speak English then they don't understand. They may not understand the words but more than likely they will know the solution to a problem and the problem is unlikely to be language.

It is an easy trap to fall into and given the Japanese style of almost always answering a question with "yes", simply asking if someone understands may lead in the wrong direction. The clues usually come in the visual nuances where it's clear someone is trying to understand what is being said. At this point, slow down and work the territory more carefully. Giving the person a chance to catch up with the conversation can lead to a significant increase in overall understanding.

Let the other speak first

Especially if you are in a leadership position, stating your opinion becomes a statement of fact that is not to be contradicted. Business society, and society in general in Japan, is one designed more for agreement and harmony than confrontation or debate.

If you need to know someone's opinion then the simplest approach is to ask them first rather than begin with "this is what I think, what do you think?" This approach will almost certainly lead to agreement that your opinion is correct and there need be little further discussion.

In fact, although you may now be under the impression that you have good ideas and everyone agrees with you, you may have lost a significant opportunity and be heading in the wrong direction. By asking for an opinion first rather than stating your own first, you eliminate the option of the person to simply agree with you and require them to outline and explain their position.

This is not something that will come naturally to a Japanese employee and will initially make them uncomfortable. But over time they'll get used to it and discussions will be significantly more productive. And you may find there are better ideas out there than you thought.

Without wanting to labor the point, this "mistake" is very common in early new starters in Japan. After a few weeks or months there will be a moment when you hear them say "Japan is so much easier than everyone said. My team agrees with everything I suggest". If you catch yourself thinking this, write it down, date the paper and come back in a year and have a laugh at your own expense.

The objective and the benefit

It is possible to simply state an instruction and expect the team or an individual to follow it. However, what is clear to one person may hold an entirely different inference for another. Simply issuing an instruction will often not achieve the desired objective. The instruction may have gone through an interpreter and the nuance or even detail may have altered. Similarly, as above, an individual may speak English to a high standard but their understanding is less comprehensive and they may not fully understand the requirement.

Ensuring everyone is aligned becomes naturally significantly more important when both language and cultural differences are taken into account. Being extremely clear on an objective has an inherent benefit that it allows all parties to clearly understand the main priority whilst at the same time essentially forcing you to think through what it is that you really want to achieve. I find this process to be actually very useful myself as it forces me to be extremely clear with myself as to what I am asking for.

By emphasizing the benefits, there is not only a reinforcement of the objectives but also provides the reason why an individual, team or company should execute a particular instruction or plan. Although this may seem obvious, and to an extent it is, the level of clarity and explanation required cannot be over emphasized.

Taking the time to clearly explain "this is what we're going to do and this is why we're going to do it" may take only a few sentences but require significant pre-planning.

I was once taught the technique that *anything can be explained in three sentences and the first one is "it's really very simple"*. If all else fails, holding to this guideline is hugely appreciated by a Japanese audience. The speaker has, in effect, taken the time and effort to consider how to concisely communicate the issue and overall comprehension is the winner.

Asking for confirmation

The possibilities for misunderstanding, although not infinite, can sometimes be relatively close. Language aside, cultural differences may lead to different interpretations; nuances such as sarcasm may be completely misconstrued and the answer to a negative question can lead to unrecognized, and unaddressed, confusion.

There is a very simple solution to this by using a conversational approach rather than asking for a "yes or no" answer. Asking a simple "do you understand?" will almost always elicit a "yes" response whether something is understood or not. *Ask the person to explain what they need to do* and very quickly it will become clear if there is a misunderstanding, or potentially a complete absence of understanding. A quick confirmation may catch a material miscommunication.

A hot temper – not cool

We've all worked with the person who has, to a lesser or greater degree, a so-called "anger management" issue. If someone is seen to regularly lose their temper then they will very rapidly become isolated and uninformed. *The policy of engagement from the staff and colleagues will quickly become one of containment.* The local team always has the option to wait out an expat, after all, their contract will be up in the next couple of years, a relatively short time in the context of an entire career.

Although we have all seen the movies where someone starts screaming and everyone in the room bows and conforms, this is the movies and not reality. Losing your cool is simply not cool. If you do tend to lapse on a regular basis, take a deep breath, remain calm and focus on the objective rather than the journey. Your team will respect you all the more for it.

The other point here is that, although positive character traits are associated with an individual, negative ones are generalized and associated with all foreigners. The person who loses their temper is tarring all foreigners with the same brush. And things can be complicated enough without that.

Rah, Rah, Rah!

The whoops and cheers that sometimes are characteristic of a style of motivational management may be something that is used in certain countries or companies. Overall though it's generally not that much of an effective approach with a Japanese workforce. It is more likely to have the effect of people forming the opinion that you may well have just arrived from Mars and reporting you to the Human Resources department.

It is often effective to end a speech with a strong statement of conviction. However it should probably avoid being delivered whilst standing on a desk and waving a hat in the air. Motivational cheerleading can be easily misinterpreted in Japan.

Here I have to give credit for trying to a good friend. In his early days in Japan he inherited a team that had seen a number of directors over a relatively short period of time. Instilling some of his natural enthusiasm he encouraged them to be outspoken and passionate about their roles. In return they encouraged him to go and see the HR Director.

Over time both parties learnt to enjoy the respective benefits of each other's style of business. It has to be said though, the entire team carries a brighter and more cheerful dynamic than it used to though still not, potentially, to the extent of standing on a desk and shouting their love for the brand!

Probably the most amusing heroic failure I've seen of this was during a company meeting one time. The president had had issues building bridges with the staff of his company and decided today was the day. Make or break. Standing in front of them he aimed for what I think may have been a "banzai" type moment. He shouted the words, punched the air and looked to the company to shout it back. And they just stood and stared. You could almost feel the underlying current flowing from them of "whatever".

Using Japanese? – avoiding the "Oops"

The Japanese for "interesting" is *omoshiroi,* and the Japanese for "looks interesting" is *omoshiroi-sou.* Similarly "tasty" is *oishii* and "looks tasty" is *oishii-sou.* Notice a pattern? However, although *kawaii* means "cute", *kawaii-sou* actually means "sad and pathetic". Always good to get a Japanese colleague to check a speech before you stand on stage.

This can become important especially when delivering hard news or aiming to motivate the team. The Japanese phrase "gambarimasu" means "I will try my best". The phrase "gambatte kudasai" means "please try your best". It would therefore seem fairly innocuous to use "gambatte kudasai" in a motivational speech to the team.

However, the nuance is significantly different as "please try your best" also implies you are not one of the team and are not holding yourself to the same expectations you have of others. Essentially it creates an "us and them" situation. Conversely the phrase "gambarimashou" means, "let's try our best". It's a statement of inclusion and oneness. A very different message.

The small differences can have significant implications. It's always worth checking the Japanese first, and with a Japanese colleague rather than a foreigner. Additionally, remember, the foreigner may enjoy setting you up but your Japanese colleagues never will.

The second issue to take into account when giving a speech is whether it will convey the essence of the message effectively. If the speaker has a strong and passionate feeling towards an issue, it works well to give the speech in their native language.

The translators will do a fine job of ensuring the actual meaning is conveyed and the audience will recognize the feeling and intensity of the speaker irrespective of whether they understand the words or not. Conveying a message in a second language is significantly harder than simply ensuring the vocabulary is correct.

Follow Up – a good idea

Especially in relation to more junior staff and often in the situation of a new foreigner as the manager, if something is unclear, *the individual is extremely unlikely to ask for clarification.* You may ask someone to perform the most simple of tasks and be surprised a day later that nothing has actually happened although the individual appeared busy all day.

I once found one of my team had spent an entire day adding up code numbers in a bank ledger, for what purpose was beyond my understanding, but they had looked the entire time industrious and productive.

It was, in reality, my own fault. As the manager I had neither confirmed the requirement was clear, nor followed up to ensure that everything was going well. A small investment in time to check everything was clearly understood would have both ensured we would have met our deadline and that the individual would have had a much more productive day.

It is easy to assume that if something is unclear to someone, they will ask however in many cases they probably won't. There is actually a cultural reason for this in that the learning process tends to be one more of observation than explanation. *Where a foreigner would tend to explain the requirement, a Japanese manager would tend to demonstrate it.*

Focus - the team rather than the individual

I once introduced what I believed would be a motivational rewards program for innovative ideas. The prize was a pair of round the world, business class tickets for the individual with the best new idea that year. They would apply for the program, have to explain their idea and what benefit it had brought to the company. Then the senior managers would decide who had won. No one applied.

The issue was, as I came to realize, no one wanted to be seen as acting as an individual rather than as a member of the team. When we changed the award to having a significantly lower monetary value but targeted it as a team award for the most innovative new idea, we had multiple applications.

Ironically, the whole concept had been developed outside Japan and we had many discussions about the objective being one to recognize individuality rather than teamwork and therefore our implementation was incorrect. However, this was more a cultural misunderstanding and we had, in fact, motivated individuals by motivating the team.

Similarly I once saw a program on a three-day race called "The Eco-Challenge". The objective was for teams of four to race over grueling country overcoming different and difficult challenges on the way. At the end of day one the US Navy Seals team had already dropped out.

At the end of day two, the Japanese team suffered an injury to one of the group who was unable to walk any further. As a group they made a decision. They didn't drop out but they picked up their injured colleague and carried her over a mountain to the finish. Being part of a group is a serious commitment in Japan.

In public, praise and feedback is best presented as a team affair rather than to an individual. The individual may feel extremely uncomfortable and often will actually resent being singled out for praise for a job well done. Their colleagues will more than likely not look too positively on the issue either and believe that the individual is attempting to place themselves before the team, whether this is the case or not. However in private they are delighted with the same words.

As a general guideline it's better to praise a team in public and an individual in private. Everyone will be more motivated that way.

Socializing with the team

An important element of Japanese corporate life whether for the most senior or for the most junior, is the act of spending regular time outside the office with co-workers. This may be in the form of simply going to a local bar for a quick drink, having dinner together or even the ever-popular karaoke sessions.

As a manager, a useful rule of thumb would be to try to socialize with staff and co-workers at least once a month (on top of all the dinners with clients and vendors). For someone just starting in Japan it is safe to err on the side of plenty and do this more often than monthly.

Socializing allows a communication channel to open between everyone that does not exist in the more formal setting of the office. It obviously allows people to approach what may be more personal questions and in their eyes the new manager is making an effort to understand them more as individuals rather than company workers and to ask questions that may not be possible to ask otherwise.

The relationships that develop are important in the context of when times are hard everyone will be there to support each other. Without this relationship it's common to see foreigners become isolated and soon this leads to being less and less effective.

The development of these relationships could also be thought of in reverse. Imagine working for a Japanese company in New York or London and being informed you were about to be assigned a new manager who had never been outside Japan and spoke no English.

Most people in this scenario would probably ensure the new manager had a fresh cup of coffee every morning and a Japanese newspaper waiting on their desk. Outside that they'd probably largely ignore them and wait for their assignment to be over. Socializing with the team allows you to break through this barrier and become a more effective and productive manager than you would be otherwise.

One of the more sensitive points about socializing with the team is that it often means there's a spouse, home alone, who may not have been prepared for this commitment to the company rather than the home and family.

Remembering the largest single cause of failure of expatriations is the spouse being unhappy with Japan and the situation they find themselves in, there is a difficult balance to strike. However, to be successful, it needs to be struck. Both the company and the family will need support.

Unfortunately, bringing a spouse to a social event with the team isn't considered generally appropriate. It's also something the local staff would rarely consider even if their spouse were to be invited. The important point to remember is that socializing with the team isn't simply analogous to going for a beer after work with the guys to relax. It's more a demonstration of your commitment to your co-workers and the company and in general it is necessary.

Hiring and Firing – the myth and the reality

The perceived wisdom about Japan is that it's almost impossible to fire an employee once they've been hired. This is considered the case even if within a probationary period. Therefore it would seem to make sense to recruit staff as temps or on short-term contracts.

The problem with taking this route is that the best candidates are rarely interested in taking short-term contracts. Additionally temp staff are typically looking for a low commitment position (though some can be excellent and may be using this as a way into a company they would like to join).

The solution to this is to hire permanent employees after a thorough review process. This may seem counter-intuitive but this is where myth and reality divide. It is possible in Japan to exit employees if approached in the correct way. In this area, as the law changes over time, it is always worth consulting a specialist on the current situation, but usually it does not need to go that far.

An employee who is not working out will generally know this to be the case already. Not only will they not be performing, they will probably not be enjoying their work either. A polite and respectful conversation to this extent will, in 99% of cases, result in the employee accepting that the best approach is for them to leave rather than have the company manage them out on a performance basis over a protracted period.

This may involve a severance payment, three months salary is not uncommon, but a senior member of staff would almost always choose to leave on good terms for the sake of future references and to avoid the drawn out divorce.

There are stories of companies that have taken action to encourage employees to leave by assigning them laborious workloads or sending them to an office in a different city. My personal view is that this is disingenuous and simply a failure of senior management to face up to the responsibility of not only managing in the good times but also in the difficult times.

Over the years I have been in the position on a number of occasions of having to exit people from different companies. In each instance, by treating the individual with respect but clearly acknowledging the reality of the situation, the person has always chosen to leave voluntarily. People are the same around the world and no one likes to be in a situation where they are not wanted. Respect is the key but effectively Japan is the same as any other country.

The only instances where I have seen issues arise and individuals go to the labor office (where the starting position is that the company is in the wrong) has been where the company has been disrespectful to the extent of being dishonest not only to the employee but also to themselves.

Taking away computers or assigning someone to the warehouse simply provokes resentment and often encourages a determination to ensure the process is as painful for the company as themselves. Treat people with respect, be clear on the situation and stay on message and the employee will, more likely than not, leave on generally good terms.

The use of lawyers – biting the hand...

Japan is not a litigious country even though its prosperity is firmly built on the foundations of the rule of law. However, laws are seen as something to be observed rather than enforced. Using a lawyer, therefore, to resolve a dispute is generally accepted to be an admission of failure.

Disputes are discussed and reconciled before ever considering turning to a legal resolution. If you find yourself in a situation where your company is in dispute, the objective should be to try every means possible to resolve the issue internally before considering the use of a lawyer.

This is partly due to the long term nature of business relationships where parties recognize they may be working together for a significant period of time, in some cases potentially their entire working lives, and therefore when questions arise, the solution is to talk rather than sue.

Moving directly to use of a lawyer without having been through the process of discussion is a genuine case of biting the hand that feeds you. The Japanese business memory is very long and using a lawyer will come back to haunt the person that does the day they need help.

Being a little too specific

I once asked our office IT technician what software had been newly loaded onto our PC's in an upgrade six months earlier. The technician, who spoke excellent English, looked at me and flatly denied there had been any upgrade six months ago.

Having had to hand over my PC for a weekend when I actually really needed it, I knew there had been an upgrade and I pressed on, a little frustrated. After about ten minutes of back and forth insistence there had and there hadn't been an upgrade about six months ago, we called a halt. The technician then asked if I'd be interested in the upgrade that had happened about eight months ago...

Although extremely frustrated, I have to admit looking back I missed all the signs that actually my initial question had been poor. I shouldn't have put a timeline into it as that simply added a new variable to be confirmed. If I'd asked about the "last" upgrade I would have eliminated an entire opportunity for misunderstanding.

Negative Questions – But didn't you say...

Negative questions cause confusion. A lot of it. The technique here is to keep your questions as simple as possible. It's a good idea to always avoid using negative questions (eg that wouldn't work would it?) the answers to which are the opposite way around in English and Japanese. So to answer the question "but didn't you say..." when the actual answer is "no" goes:

- English   - no I didn't

- Japanese   - yes, I didn't

Avoid asking negative questions but listen out for yourself doing it. It's so engrained in English usage it's a hard habit to break.

Negative questions are second nature in the English language but a bad habit in the context of business in Japan. The aim is to avoid negative questions and convert any inquiry into a positive format wherever possible. Then the English and Japanese responses are consistent and confusion is avoided.

The second habit that we all have on arrival in Japan is to accept an answer at face value. The key is to ensure that you really understand the question you've asked in the first place. Keep it simple, avoid negative questions and avoid detail that might not be absolutely necessary. And remember that when a Japanese person says "yes", it might just mean "no".

Interestingly, negative questions are also very common in Japanese but there is something in the translation, whether perceived or real, that causes this confusion. They are simply best avoided.

Bowing – being polite without embarrassment

Bowing is a very respectful gesture in Japan that has been developed to a fine art. And a foreigner is never going to get it quite right.

A wonderful example of the politeness inherent in Japanese society I find is the snack ladies on the Shinkansen. All day they walk up and down the center aisle of the train selling snacks and beer to weary salarymen and excited children. And each time they leave each carriage they turn and bow to the passengers before moving on to start the process again in the next car.

Another example is to look out of your plane's window as it pulls back from the gate at Narita Airport. You'll see the ground crew politely bowing to the aircraft. This one makes a great photograph. Watch out for it, you won't see this level of politeness in many other countries.

People bow for many reasons and in many different ways. The good news though is that foreigners won't be expected to get it right so don't need to try to emulate their colleagues. Rather, resort to a courteous nod of the head and form will have been fulfilled.

I still shudder at the memories of when I first arrived in Japan and tried to execute a full ninety-degree bow to some of the senior members of my new company. It brought much appreciation but not a little hilarity from the gentlemen who never failed to light heartedly remind me of it over any and all beers in the months (and years) to come.

Bowing, and a general recognition of respect, is important and a simple Western style nod of the head will satisfy this requirement. You'll recognize the times this will be necessary, for example on exchanging meishi (business cards), at the end of a meeting or saying goodbye to someone.

After a while, so the old joke goes, you'll find yourself nodding on the phone as well. The only thing is that it's not actually a joke. You probably will catch yourself after a few months doing exactly that!

What exactly did he say?

We are all guilty of hearing what we would like to hear. The reality as a manager though, when language, culture and backgrounds are different, is that this may become a genuine inhibition to success. A company that rotates the senior positions around countries on a bi-annual basis, as some still do, are, to all intents and purposes, ensuring that the value of the learning curve is rarely leveraged.

If you are reading this book it is likely you are new to Japan and, although you may have significant experience in the company or sector itself, you may still be learning the art of understanding what you are hearing.

The obvious examples of this are the responses to negative questions however a simple misplaced yes or no, may disguise a complete lack of appreciation of a situation. When listening, the result may be very different from that which you may have been expecting.

Anything confidential is an "open" secret

As in all business experiences, people tend to talk. A "confidential" discussion can soon become a point of office gossip without much assistance and the more confidential, the greater the degree that human nature drives someone to discuss it. And, as a foreigner, everything you say or do is a magnified point of interest to your co-workers.

The issue for the new arrival in Japan is that they are out of the loop on office gossip. They don't casually pick up on the water cooler conversations and they aren't included in chain of conversation as it spreads around a building. There is also the added effect of people asking each other for clarification as anything they will have said will almost always have been said in a language other than Japanese, either with or without a translator.

The key is not to assume that everything remains confidential simply because you are not hearing about it. You're not hearing about it because you don't speak Japanese and being a foreigner are probably kept further from open conversations than would otherwise be the case. I find it useful to assume that, unless there is a specific and enforceable embargo on information remaining confidential, it will be relatively widely know in a short period of time. *Nothing travels faster than confidential information!*

Do I need to speak Japanese to work in Japan?

No. But sometimes it does help. Especially outside Tokyo. I have friends in Tokyo who have lived here more than twenty years and can still barely direct a taxi in Japanese. The reality is that if you can recognize the cultural nuances of what is happening around you and can respond to them appropriately, this is often more important than actually being able to understand the words themselves. That is, *it is more effective to invest a little time in learning Japanese people than a lot of time in studying the Japanese language.* Especially for a short stay of two or three years.

However, it is certainly a limitation if you are planning to work outside the gaishikei (foreign branded company) environment. Foreign companies are designed to accommodate the peculiarities of the foreign and Japanese interaction. Additionally, Japanese at a gaishikei have typically chosen to work in the environment and enjoy the differences from a traditional domestic company.

However, a domestic company is not typically set up to accommodate a foreigner with limited Japanese and little experience of working in the culture. This is a generalization as in certain circumstances, for example for a financial or technical specialist, companies can very successfully intertwine a non-Japanese speaker into their operations but outside the gaishikei and financial business it would not be straightforward for them to play a productive role in their work.

Interestingly there are, in some instances, advantages to being a non-speaker (or at least being perceived to be a non-Japanese speaker). Speaking English with authority and passion will lead to significantly greater effect and response from a Japanese team than attempting two years of painful, poorly pronounced Japanese. *The point can be translated, the emotion and intensity, not.*

I have also seen the reverse though where a foreigner who speaks almost no Japanese will go out of their way in front of their colleagues from head office to use very simple Japanese when they are around. This works on the basis that the person from head office understands zero Japanese and will assume the person is fluent when in reality they were probably hardly understood at all. Still looks good on the old report card to the boss overseas.

The extended pause and the sound of silence

In Japanese business there are often extended pauses in a conversation. This is partly style and partly an open display of someone considering all angles before continuing with a discussion. This can actually be quite disconcerting when experienced for the first time. A foreigner would tend to want to fill the void of what could be perceived as an uncomfortable silence.

The important point here is that a long pause is simply part of the style of conversation in Japan and nothing more. It may feel uncomfortable but foreigners soon get used to this as they become more attuned to Japan. Don't try to fill the gap or infer from it that there is an ulterior motive at play.

A good example of this dates from the 1980s when the president of major US computer company came to Japan to sign a major deal with one of Japan's airlines. The deal had been under negotiation for several months and represented a major coup for the American business. As the two presidents sat side by side for the signing ceremony, the American turned to his Japanese counterpart and remarked "Great deal, huh?" to which the Japanese president did not immediately reply.

Interpreting this as a sign that the Japanese customer was not actually happy with the terms, and before waiting for a reply, the American became uncomfortable with the silence and offered to drop the price. The highly experienced businessman had misread the situation, got the deal but gave away a significant sum for no other reason than he was uncomfortable with a momentary silence.

There is however a balance to be made. When I first arrived in Japan I'd been told about long pauses and not to be uncomfortable with them. I'd started to experience this almost as soon as I arrived and was becoming quite comfortable with not trying to fill the gaps. At dinner one night I remember being with the president of the company I was working for. He was renown for his long pauses between remarks and, being prepared, I sat quietly through them until he continued the conversation. However, after one particularly long silence, he looked at me and said, "You don't say very much, do you".

Speaking English – is it that difficult?

One of the first surprises for many starting a career in Japan is the lack of basic English skills for a modern country. Or any country for that matter. Anyone completing high school will have received a minimum of eight years of English lessons and yet most struggle to order a beer in a bar. The school curriculum has focused on ensuring an exam pass by teaching grammar and vocabulary but almost nothing on spoken communication skills.

The result is the low level of English ability today, which is seen by many in Japanese industry itself as a major problem for Japan's future in an internationally integrated world.

In 2011 Rakuten (a large on-line retailer) announced the working language of the company would be English. So the story goes, Mikitani-san, the founder and CEO stood up at a company meeting and said "from now on, all meetings will be in

English". Asked when this new policy was to take effect he looked at the individual and said "now".

Mikitani-san noted that inside the company this caused problems that took significant time and resource to resolve and in many cases younger, more aggressive learners were taking the positions of their more senior, but mono-lingual, colleagues. He also noted though that communication with the overseas elements of business had significantly improved and problems that might have taken days or weeks to resolve by email were now resolved by a ten minute phone call. Internationalization was the way to go and English was the engine.

Having worked for a number of international brands, I've witnessed the usual approach to solving this dilemma of investing heavily into English lessons for the staff. In a number of cases the investment has been as high as 1% of annual sales, a major commitment. And the English ability has stayed stubbornly constant. Group lessons are the most common form, aiming to include as many as possible with the limited resource available.

The problem is that this fails to address motivation or the simple fact that it's been tried in their high school days for eight years and clearly didn't work. A more targeted and creative approach is necessary.

At a department off-site once, I asked everyone present what they wanted to be doing in five years time. Most replied with the usual mix of looking to have gained a promotion in that time but one stood out. He said he wanted to work in the global head office of our company to see how an international business is really run. This took me completely by surprise and, as a result, I committed fully to supporting his objective.

We talked for some time and agreed that his skills were close to the level required and that professionally he was ready to make the transfer. I had the necessary contacts and could have arranged the transfer immediately if we'd wanted too. The elephant in the corner though was his English ability. It simply wasn't up to the standard required and I'd have been setting him up for failure if I'd pushed ahead too soon.

So we agreed on a timeline of eighteen months to two years to bring his English skills up and to work with the global team on ensuring the right placement. The key issue, as is common in the Japanese work place, is conversational English and this is what we focused on.

On his own initiative he joined an American basketball team and, playing with them twice a week, hung out at the end of the game and had a beer with the boys. After eighteen months his English was conversational, he transferred to the head office, eventually taking a permanent role and stayed there successfully for over ten years.

He now speaks native Japanese, fluent English and very good German. *All from having a beer with the guys.*

The point here is to focus. There needs to be a motivational element to learning such as restrictions on promotions or grades until a certain standard has been achieved or only allowing fluent speakers to travel to international meetings (and thereby limiting the exposure required to make a successful career in an international business).

The issue at the moment is that training budgets tend to be thinly spread and applied in a time-honored fashion that has been proven not to work. Instead, they are much more effective employed on targeted individuals with a strong motivation to learn and use English behind them.

A good example of this relates to another manager working in the same company as the one above. He was ready in all aspects to make a jump in his career and in many ways was the ideal person for the role. Except that it required international communication and his spoken English simply wasn't there. So his manager arranged for him to spend three months on secondment in Australia.

He came back to Japan, speaking good communication level English, to a promotion to the role he'd been targeting. Within a year was promoted once again. There was less money to go around for the normal English classes but we had a success that would otherwise not have been there. And a very good international manager in the process. And a good example to the non-English speakers of the direct benefits to themselves of making the transition from domestic to international. Be creative with training budgets, throwing money at lessons is often a wasted time and resource.

What happened to the company car?

Many countries, in Europe especially, provide a company car to some or all of their employees. Historically this came around due to tax laws where is was more beneficial for the company and the individual to provide a car than pay a higher salary and let the individual buy the car themselves. Originally this may have been the case but it has become entrenched and many employees see it as a simple part of the expected package, needed or not.

One of the countries that does not typically provide company cars though is Japan. Living in the major cities with the excellent transport infrastructure there is hardly any need for a car (though with kids it becomes easier with one) but the key issue is parking.

To own a car the individual requires proof of parking and the company would have to find significant and expensive parking at the office as well. Most would prefer the extra income and many, having no need of owning vehicle, would really not appreciate one.

The one exception to this is the company president. It is relatively common amongst the international brands that the president would have a company car for the daily commute to the office and also have parking available when they arrive if they choose to travel this way.

For the foreign companies there is no fixed requirement of the type of vehicle for the president. Most simply inherit the previous incumbent's vehicle or choose a car they like with budgets ranging from Peugeots to Mercedes.

If you are in the position of choosing a new car as part of your package, it's common to look at the international brands, something that has been on the wanted list for many years but never available at company expense until now. Before signing the contract though, it's worth looking at both the domestic brands and the used car market.

The domestic brands such as Toyota, Nissan or Honda will most likely provide a vehicle with more gadgets and specs on it than will the international brands for the same price.

The separate point around the used market is that many wealthy Japanese will change cars on an almost annual basis. The quality will be like new and the price will be a fraction of the original sticker price. You just might be able to afford the S-Class instead of the C-Class.

The final point when choosing a company car is that, without going too ridiculous, the car of the president can be an aspirational choice the staff will look to. It may seem at first sight that choosing a budget car is sending a good message however, this can also be seen in reverse.

An employee at the beginning of their career, looking at the low end car being driven by the president, may just think to themselves "is that it?". Their view is that they're looking to work for twenty years and an old banger is not exactly what they are looking forward to. Examples are set in many directions.

Offshoring and Japanese speaking staff

I once bravely embarked on an outsourcing program that was to take approximately fifty positions from within the company I was working at and placing them overseas. The concept was that no positions that were in direct contact with customers would be touched but simple data entry roles were fair game.

The savings over three years would be approximately 30% of the cost if the positions remained in-house. Communication would be maintained easily through telephone and email. Weekly status review meetings were also in place amongst the senior teams to ensure quality control aspects were addressed on a timely basis.

Post event I was asked if I would do this again in the future. This drew a very long pause. My actual answer was "no". Although we'd achieved a significant element of the savings we'd originally targeted, the non-quantifiable disruption to the business more than offset the benefits gained from the process. At least that is what I believed.

To start, offshoring and outsourcing is possible. There are many global companies that offer these services predominantly transferring the workload to China or India. In our case we opted for a city some two hours outside Shanghai on the basis that the outsource company had a material presence there and that the local university was producing thousands of Japanese graduates annually.

Excluding the normal pushback that will be experienced in any outsourcing process, the benefits of the project were undermined by two distinctly Japanese issues. There were additional problems arising from issues on both sides however I will focus on the two that will be universally encountered if an offshoring project is initiated.

Firstly language. We recruited only Chinese staff that had graduated with a Japanese language degree. Even so, the language ability was not at a native standard. The optimal word here being "native". Although I could converse without a problem with the entire team in Japanese, I am used to foreigners speaking Japanese and therefore relatively accustomed to hearing errors and being able to accommodate them.

Internally, this was also true for the majority of the Japanese team within the company however the problems arose around the minority that did not have this experience. For them, working with a sub-native level of Japanese became increasingly frustrating which led to an overall decline in the reputation of the offshore team. Fairly or unfairly that was the situation and the wisdom of the entire process was brought into question. More and more the requirement for native speakers rather than fluent Japanese speakers became a recurring issue.

The second point arose from the difference between the two groups' level of attention to detail. For the Japan team everything had to necessarily be spot on. This seems a very reasonable requirement though when we had started the company a decade before it had been every man for himself as we learned the new processes. However, at this stage the company was well established and the expectation was for accuracy from day one.

There is a learning curve though and with the best will in the world, everyone starts at the bottom. As a result the training stages of the project, that had been planned as a matter of weeks, extended into a matter of months until the Japan team was comfortable that the new people were ready to take on their roles. This pushed the entire project further back which then impacted upon other follow-on processes to be rolled in and so on.

We did eventually reduce overall costs in this project but neither ourselves, nor the partner company, were completely happy with the results. If a company is considering outsourcing from Japan, the intangible costs should be clearly identified in advance and the senior management aligned to take the rough with the smooth.

The alternative to outsourcing is "in-sourcing" whereby an external company places its own people within the organization. We applied this in IT, Finance, Logistics and Design. In these instances we brought in local specialists but from outside companies. They had their own place and effectively became part of the team over time.

This proved to be significantly more successful than either outsourcing or relying on third parties for specific roles where they are not based permanently in the office. This I would do again. Off-shoring, big question mark.

Outsourcing – it even comes in English

As opposed to offshoring, Japan has an excellent supply of English language outsourcing support for all matters whether personal or corporate. There is even a new business model around virtual outsourcing via the internet where you never actually meet the people involved. You can have a virtual assistant who will make all those bookings for you, arrange your schedule and keep track of your contacts and business cards and you will never actually know if they are real or not.

Until recently the main issue had been one of English language. Large companies could always call on vendors to provide a more expensive English support but for smaller companies, the cost of this had been prohibitive.

Over the last decade though there has been an increase in both the language skill set and also boutique business offering any manner of outsourcing. This started in IT and HR and has now spread to almost all back office functions and, with the increase in supply, the prices have fallen significantly.

If a supplier cannot provide the English language support you require, you can now change your supplier. Until recently this really wasn't straightforward.

Off-sites – and why everyone will object

There are two types of off-site meeting. The small focused one, potentially with a department or a senior management team. The benefits of isolating these groups to focus on a specific issue for a period of uninterrupted time are well recognized and many companies use them to accelerate development of an idea or project.

The second type of off-site is less utilized but potentially far more far-reaching and involves effectively taking an entire company to a remote location for a two to three day session of training, communication and the inevitable team building.

Company off-sites are a significant undertaking with potentially hundreds of employees leaving their regular roles and becoming part of a directed corporate message. These off-sites are particularly effective at communicating simple corporate messages that need to be promulgated throughout the entire organization such as a new corporate strategy or a key global message. They also provide an opportunity to communicate informally with the staff through evening or early morning activities.

The key to a successful off-site is to know precisely the message the organization must walk away with when the event is complete and focusing all activity around this. This can be in the form of presentations but usually more effectively through various activities to underscore the point being communicated.

In Japan there are many event companies that will assist in this however they tend to be either event organizers, ie a company focused on locating the facility, providing the entertainment and coordinating the flow, or an activity company that provides the actual content for each element of the off-site. This means you will need to not only create the core message to be delivered but also work with two separate teams to execute a really successful off-site.

Once an off-site has been announced, be prepared for the reasons why almost everyone will be unable to attend. The excuses and critical reasons will be endless. This though is simply human nature, the staff are unsure of why they are being told to give up their regular routine for one or two nights, they don't like the concept of being away from their families or they simply don't like the idea of being with their colleagues, especially overnight.

This is normal. Almost everyone will have a reason why they can't go and it will be up to the senior management team to stand together and enforce the event. This concern will also be almost universally reversed at the end of the event with everyone having understood and enjoyed it and be looking forward to the next. There will always be some who remains set against the event even if they actually enjoyed it but these will be in a small minority. At one event I organized in Fukushima Prefecture in 2012, over 500 staff attended, many/most of who had held severe reservations beforehand however in the post event surveys there was one solitary individual who said they would never do this again.

Off-sites are not necessarily unusual in the Japanese corporate context but nor are they the norm. People will genuinely be concerned about being away from families and unless planned properly with a clear core concept, everyone may walk away no wiser for having attended.

The core message is key, keep it simple, define the two or three points that the attendees should walk away not only remembering but believing and motivated to achieve. Use different activities to reinforce this rather than relying on two days of PowerPoint. And always remember the party on the last night, give everyone a chance to let their hair down.

One caveat, it is highly unlikely temporary staff will be allowed by their employment company to join. The temp agencies tend to take the view that unless a "benefit" can be provided to all their employees, and not just those working for a specific company, then the staff cannot participate. This is a fight not worth fighting, ask once and if the answer is no, move on, you have other things to focus on and you're not going to win.

Off-sites will receive enormous pushback from the company when first announced but are generally very effective. And there is no reason to limit the attendance to employees only. Over the years I have many times included key business partners and accounts. It's an opportunity to further relations with them too. However, it's always an idea to limit third parties to some extent or staff will feel they need to spend their time looking after them rather than joining the activities.

The effort involved in organizing a successful event cannot be underestimated. Once the purpose has been defined it won't simply organize itself. A thousand decisions will need to be made and every aspect of the process will need to be reviewed.

Someone who is good at thinking laterally should be appointed to lead the project. And that person should be an empowered member of the senior team. Everyone is going to have an opinion on what should be included but only one person can actually be held to deliver. That person must have the authority to say "no" when the time comes.

I once organized an event for several hundred employees. A key aspect was to ensure that, during the breakout activities in smaller groups, everyone would be with new people and not just their best friends. We wanted the attendees broken into six large groups and then within these groups they should be broken into six smaller teams. To do this we decided to use colored t-shirts to split into six big teams and then numbers on the t-shirts to define the smaller groups.

When reviewing the detail I found that my organization team had decided to randomize the groups themselves. To do this they planned to use the corporate organization chart to define who received which color and what number. They would then arrange for the correct t-shirts to be in the correct rooms when everyone arrived. A colossal amount of work.

I suggested we split the shirts by size (small, medium and large), threw all the shirts the same size into three very large boxes and then have people select a shirt as they walked into the main hall in the morning. Not knowing the purpose for the color or mix ensured a random take up and the workload was reduced by 99%.

This is a simple example but multiplied many times defines the difference between a successful and a labored event. Put a senior decision maker in charge of the event rather than simply passing it to more junior staff and hoping it will work. It will make all the difference in the world. As mentioned, the content of the off-site should be varied to maximize the benefit of the exercise. At one recent event we included:

- An introduction and purpose of the days by the President
- A history of the brands present
- An exercise in teamwork creating large wooden puzzles
- Group think processes followed by team presentations on their ideas
- Early morning training
- Group voting systems to prioritize ideas and concepts
- A ballet troupe
- Taiko drums to call everyone to order
- A great party split across four areas including music, live acts, relaxation therapy and a quiet room that remained quiet.

The options are limitless, they should just include more than three days of PowerPoint.

Long vacations – or any vacation

Long vacations are rare in Japan and any vacation tends to be taken as focused and intense short periods of activity. One way to fracture the relationship with a team very quickly is to take a long vacation especially soon after arriving in Japan. In reality this has to be considered from the staff's point of view. Most will only receive ten to fifteen days vacation allowance each year and will probably only take half of these days in any case.

For the team it's a sign of commitment to company and dedication to supporting each other. From this perspective it is quite easy to understand the resentment caused when a new foreigner is transferred in and the first thing they do is take three weeks vacation. As a general guideline, it's a good idea to avoid vacation for the first few months and be aware of the implications with the team if taking longer time off.

Although the automatic response may be to consider vacation as a private matter, this is actually more serious than might appear at first sight. Over the years I've witnessed a number of failed expatriations where the cause of the breakdown related to long vacations being taken when the team believed it was inappropriate.

True it's not actually the business of the team and the vacation is probably something that was clearly discussed prior to the move to Japan, but unless opinions are taken into account, the time in Japan may be shorter than expected.

Expatriates genuinely do need their vacation to maintain stress levels below critical (they are learning a new culture and living in a new language after all). However, as with many other aspects of working here, there is a team dynamic involved that needs to be considered. And yes, someone probably is watching their Facebook page and the vacation may be significantly more public than expected.

The art of working through a translator

I was once in a presentation being given by a new foreigner to Japan. He was the new Marketing Director and giving his first speech to the combined Sales and Marketing teams, some hundred plus people all together. About ten minutes into the presentation he turned and shouted at one of the girls, telling her to shut up while he was talking. She looked up a little surprised and replied "but I'm the translator".

It is very likely that if you are in the first months or even years of being an expatriate in Japan, you will necessarily be working through a translator, whether a professional one or simply someone in the office who speaks good English which brings its own set of issues.

Working through a translator is a skill in its own right. Humor no longer works as, even if through a translator with an excellent sense of comedy, timing is no longer guaranteed. One-liners that may be highly amusing when you say them, simply fall flat as the audience hears a literal translation of your words. The point that is still valid though is that your tone and intensity remain, even though the words themselves cannot be understood.

For this reason it's always a good option to work through a translator for a speech even in the instance you would like to try presenting in Japanese. The translator will take care of the message and the audience will hear your voice and passion.

As with any new person working in a company, a translator needs time to absorb the specific language and vocabulary of the business. As a result many companies go to great lengths to ensure that they use the same translator each time to the extent of rescheduling meetings and events if the person is unavailable.

Generally speaking, there are two types of translator. Those who provide literal translation and those who provide the colloquial word. The literal ones are excellent for technical meetings when it is the detail that is important. The colloquial ones are perfect when the situation requires a softer touch and it is the feeling of the words rather than their literal interpretation that is important such as at a business dinner where it is the relationship rather than the subject that is important.

If you ever find a translator that is good at both literal and colloquial interpretation, hire them before someone else does.

Contact with the yakuza – leave it to others

The *yakuza* (the Japanese equivalent of the Mafia) tend to leave foreign companies alone to a large extent. However, if your business includes a significant retail element, and therefore property and the such like, it is possible that you may become a target for yakuza funding. Usually there will be a request for a "community service fee" with the distinct message of "pay up or face the consequences".

The police are unlikely to provide much assistance in these cases, they've been allowing the yakuza to continue their business for several hundred years after all. Additionally they tend to be focused on resolving rather than preventing crime. At the time of the Aum attacks I was working at a foreign company in Tokyo. One day we received an unmarked package and were at a loss as to whether to open it or not. Resolving to take it to the local police, when we arrived, we were advised to return to our office, taking the package with us. If we opened it and found a bomb or poison gas, would we then return and let them know. Not really the assistance we were looking for.

Typically the best approach is allow one of the senior Japanese in your company manage the situation. They will understand the implications and be able to resolve the issue in a very Japanese way. This is one where the foreigner is more likely to be a liability than an asset. And additionally, do you really want them knowing who you are?

Working with a bilingual computer – don't do it

In something over twenty years I have yet to find a simple and stable bilingual solution to a computer so that it can switch seamlessly between English and Japanese. Both Windows and Mac provide a good basis for this in relation to email, web-browsing and word documents but none excels at providing complete platform inter-operability when an application is in one language or the other.

Loading two operating systems onto one machine is simply asking for trouble and always leads to regular crashes and data loss.

These days computers (both Windows and Mac) can manage the different character sets of English and Japanese quite well. It's possible to read and in some cases type both languages and this should cover most of the requirement so it no longer becomes a necessity to be able to switch between the two at a menu level. You can read the email, or at least your assistant can read it to you, so effectively job done.

The second issue with trying to use a Japanese computer for working in English is the question of keyboard. The layout is different between the two, Japanese having significantly less requirement for a space bar for example (there being no spaces between Japanese text). This makes typing in English a little disconcerting and if you have an English computer at home then regularly switching between the two is even more confusing.

The solution is just to use what you are used to. If you are used to an English keyboard then simply tell the IT team to get you one. They will be able to do it although they may claim it's not possible. And if they can't do it, you need a new IT team.

As an aside to this, when purchasing a computer in Japan for personal use it can be quite difficult to find one with an English language operating system. This is actually quite understandable as 99% plus of machines sold will be to domestic consumers. And they want Japanese.

For Windows, the back streets of Akihabara are the best bet. There are stores that specialize in servicing the expatriate community and will be able to provide English operating system and keyboard as well as some basic software.

However, for Mac it is much simpler. At any Apple store (the actual Apple stores, not a retailer who sells Macs) you can simply ask them to change the keyboard to English. It'll take about twenty minutes and they'll happily take your phone number and call you when it's ready. The Mac will then boot up and you can choose which language you'd like it to work in and it becomes a native language machine.

Designer stubble – it often doesn't work

I was once at a presentation of do's and don'ts in Japanese business. Much of it was very basic and some even simply wrong where the presenter had misunderstood a situation. On the whole I'd like that ninety minutes of my life back as it was pretty much an utter waste of time but towards the end, one final issue caught my attention.

We were shown a picture of the executives from the head office of a foreign company coming to Japan and making a formal apology at a press conference for something their local subsidiary had been involved with.

The picture of the three executives was held up and we were asked to identify what they were doing that was causing great offence to the audience at the meeting. We all looked at the picture and couldn't see anything wrong. The executives were extremely well attired, carrying the appropriate look of contrition and had clearly been trained on personal presentation. We gave up.

The presenter then turned and pointed at one of the three in the picture who had immaculately prepared designer stubble. It looked expensive and probably took some significant time each day to maintain. "Look," said our presenter with an excited jab of the finger, "he forgot to shave".

The concept of designer stubble, no matter how well presented, simply isn't understood in Japan. It's clean-shaven or a beard, no half way measures or people will simply think you forgot to shave in the morning.

The Places People Play

In Tokyo there is really only one place for a new foreigner to look for both socializing and networking, the Tokyo American Club (TAC). Next to the Russian embassy in Roppongi, TAC has been completely redeveloped from the ground up and re-opened in 2010 following a number of years in a temporary facility near Shinagawa. TAC has excellent sports and social facilities and organizes regular business functions and presentations and is very good for the new arrival to find their feet in Japan.

However, TAC isn't the only place in town. The British Club, having expired many years ago, left a hole that has partly been filled through and expansion of the Foreign Correspondents Club of Japan, FCCJ. This is a business networking club with meeting and dining facilities and is aimed squarely at the business community. It's target is not the family, having no social facilities, but simply a lot of interesting people with a wide and diverse background.

Out of Tokyo, in Yokohama, there is the Yokohama Country and Athletics Club (YCAC), one of the oldest establishments for foreigners in Japan. Located in Naka-ku, with sports fields, tennis courts and a clubhouse, YCAC is squarely aimed at the social side of living in Japan. Sister to the Kobe Regatta and Athletic Club (KRAC) in Kansai, it dates back to the early days of the foreign community originally located in Yokohama (where the government could keep and eye on them).

Located in Hiroo, The Tokyo Lawn Tennis Club harks back to 1900. Although the official title is one of lawn tennis, these days it sports clay courts rather than grass. Focused on the tennis enthusiast, this is a club for both social and business networking.

On the more corporate entertainment side, Roppongi Hills sports an excellent club on the 51st floor with some of the finest evening views of Tokyo to be found. The facilities consist of a main bar and various restaurants and is very much aimed at the business community, children not being allowed apart from at the weekend. The view though is spectacular.

Finally there is the Tokyo Club. If you don't know what this is, you probably shouldn't.

Getting a driver – possible but...

In many countries in Asia, China, Korea, Indonesia for example, it is fairly normal practice for the expatriate to have a company employed, full time driver. In both China and Korea it is mandated by many foreign companies to use one and the expat is often not allowed to drive as a term of his or her contract for insurance purposes. However drivers are low cost and relatively common in those countries.

This isn't the case in Japan. It is possible to have a full time driver but they're going to be paid at full time employee rates. This would mean, given the overtime a driver will most likely incur, that the annual cost is going to be in excess of ¥5million ($50,000), probably quite a bit in excess of it in fact.

As a result, few foreign brands still retain the company driver and simply use a taxi or hire service as and when required. The large Japanese companies, banks, trading houses and the like, still retain the drivers but this is very much a question of status rather than convenience. If one president has a driver, the next isn't going to give his own up.

Work visas – if you're going to Shinagawa?

Assuming all the paperwork is complete, actually obtaining a working visa in Japan usually means an arduous journey to the immigration center. It also means long queues and hours of waiting. It is possible to find an outsource service for this but the process can be expensive and inconsistent with the advice they provide often being old and out of date.

There is however an alternative to this. Although your assistant won't thank me for telling you, there is a one-day course that they can attend at the Ministry of Justice to become qualified to provide visa services. They are allowed to prepare the documents on your behalf and also to both file the application and collect the visa when it is issued.

It currently costs around ¥30,000 to become qualified but as an expat, your time of going halfway across town and waiting in line is very likely to cost more than that anyway. A good overall investment, and you can tell your assistant they are improving their skill set and career prospects. They still won't be happy to go all the way to the other side of Shinagawa though.

Golf – the ultimate corporate game

The stereotype of the golf mad Japanese corporate executive is not so much a stereotype as actually true. A day on the links is considered vital to the good development of business relations and to turn down an invitation something of a slap in the face.

Many Japanese executives and non-executives alike are outstanding golfers and will regularly spend an entire weekend on the course; lunch being mandatory, the minimum is a day.

There are courses all across Japan though from Tokyo the nearest are more than an hour's drive. Play can start early in the morning and after the front nine there will inevitably be lunch at the clubhouse. The back nine will then be followed by a trip to the onsen, possibly dinner and then the return home. Golf is serious business in Japan. I've actually played in a typhoon and my colleagues looked at me in horror when I suggested we should shelve the day as there was a risk we could be killed in the storm.

It is not actually necessary to play golf in Japan, but it is an excellent way to build relations with colleagues and partners if you do. Having a usual score of around 120, I'm generally not considered to be playing the game and so provide a face saving reason why my colleague should attend rather than myself. It does seem to provide several extra vacation days a year to those who are serious about the game though.

Weddings and the corporate account

It is traditional at a Japanese wedding to present the happy couple with a gift of ¥30,000~50,000 ($300~500). It is also traditional that the manager attend the wedding and more than likely make a speech at the ensuing party.

Effectively the manager is tied into an obligation that is going to cost him or her a significant amount over the years. It's therefore a matter of corporate policy as to whether these funds can be charged on expenses. My personal view is yes, however it is purely a matter of policy and there is no legal or traditional background to this. It's a relatively small sum for a corporate expense account but much appreciated by the manager and looks positive for the company.

There are also other traditional amounts that the company picks up, the most obvious being Condolence Money. These amounts are usually defined in a companies work rules but have been included again as a matter of policy rather than any legislative requirement. The amounts typically depend on how close the unfortunate individual is to the company. It would be most for an actual employee but also there may be a contribution for a spouse or direct relative. Beyond one degree of freedom a company would tend not to provide any additional funding.

So why can't I drive to work?

It is not uncommon in Japan for a company to include in its work rules the requirement for employees to use public transport to the office. This, rather onerous requirement, comes from the belief that a company may be liable for any injuries incurred when driving to or from the office.

Although legal advice should potentially be sought as things do change over time, I have always had this clause removed when I find it at a company. I take the view that it is somewhat ridiculous that a company should be liable for the behavior of its employees anywhere other than in the work place (outside issues of corporate reputation of course). If an employee is drunk on the bus and starts a fight, to me that is just as relevant as if they were driving their car and carelessly drove into a wall.

When I reviewed the situation on this I actually found that many employees were driving to work but simply parked away from the office and walked the last few hundred meters. The issue was clearly ridiculous and a quick change of the work rules allowed people to be less covert about their daily commute. It also allowed over twenty employees who regularly rode their bicycles secretly to the office, to have a safe and guarded place in the car park to keep them.

The office romance – are they or aren't they?

You will never know about it. However, this isn't because you're missing the signals sent in Japanese, it's because no one else in the office will know about it either. Japanese don't generally socialize as a couple; even if they're out with friends in a karaoke box together they would not typically acknowledge each other, remaining separate through the evening and meeting secretly once everyone has gone home.

This obviously isn't a problem if you're married but if you're young and single then you probably would prefer to know if the girl of your dreams is about to get married to someone else. And to get in there quick before it's too late. Sorry, can't help you on this one but be prepared for a possible polite, but unexplained, rejection; she might be dating the guy sitting next to you.

I once asked why people were so secretive of relationships in Japan. Interestingly, the answer was not that it was no one else's business but almost relating to an economic valuation. My Japanese friend explained to me that her value could be considered one hundred if she were seen to be single, fall to fifty if she was known to be dating, and drop to zero once she was married with children. If you are wondering, the person who explained this to me was herself a successful Japanese career woman, and seemingly single. Though maybe not.

Expatriation failures – and how to avoid them

The biggest single cause of an expatriation failure is not the expat themselves but rather their spouse not settling in Japan. It is significantly easier to adapt to Japan when you have a focus and reason to get up every day. The small issues that can become annoying if you let them are overlooked and the day has a purpose to it. However, the spouse is often not supported by the company and has to proactively develop a life for themselves.

A number of the international schools offer mentoring support which can provide some of the focus that alleviates the stress of living in a new society. However it's up to the spouse themselves to reach out for this and wouldn't typically be available if there are no children.

Those who find themselves in the position of being without a strong purpose in Japan, are not the first and certainly won't be the last. There are clubs and activities outside the Tokyo American Club and there is a great option to start to learn Japanese. Learning kanji can be remarkably therapeutic and helps you find your way around at the same time. The key is not to simply sit at home and think that everything in the country is difficult or just plain wrong and that it's time to return to the familiarity and comfort of your home country. It really will be missing out on a wonderful experience.

For the expat themselves, they should be aware of the situation of the spouse. Often the new role will require late nights and dinners with business partners. It's always important to try to strike a balance and be aware that the spouse may actually be experiencing greater stress without something to do than the expatriate is in their new position.

Overtime - when they don't want to go home

One of the issues about working life in Japan is how late people stay in the office. This is for a multitude of reasons including peer pressure despite the company requesting that staff leave early. Alternatively it could be the manager is still at their desk. This tacitly implies everyone else should also still be there too (if you are the manager reading this at your desk, it's time to go home). Or it could simply be a desire not to return home at all.

However, it is a major problem from the perspective of work-life balance as well as employee health and welfare. Burning the midnight oil is necessary sometimes however when 50% of your staff are working past 10.00PM every day, this isn't healthy or quite possibly even legal. But it is very common.

To address this is extremely difficult and I have tried many times over many years though rarely been more than mildly successful. The simple "well, just tell them to go home" will usually result in smiles from the other managers around.

Ask ten people why they're working late and you'll hear ten different answers as to why it's absolutely critical they complete the work tonight or the project will fail (and by implication, it'll be your fault). The reality of course is that any work after about 9.00PM probably isn't the highest quality and the first two hours the next morning will be spent correcting it.

At one company I worked at, we once instituted a "lights out" policy. It was announced within the company that lights and air conditioning would be switched off at 8.00PM every night. The objective was clearly to actually force the staff to leave the office. We'd tried everything else already.

We presented the new policy at a company meeting a month in advance of go-live. We issued a reminder two weeks before its introduction and another the day before. At 7.50PM on the first day of implementation we announced over the office PA system lights were about to go out in ten minutes and on the dot of 8.00 the building went dark.

And then the screams from the ladies bathroom started and we had to switch the lights back on. People simply hadn't taken it seriously that this was going to happen.

The second day went a little better and most people had left the building following the 7.50 announcement and over the next few weeks things seemed to start to improve in general. The same work was being performed but in less time, and people were getting out earlier to head home to their families.

Then I found out that some of staff had been renting a nearby karaoke bar and simply carrying on there! After a few more weeks small desk lights started to appear and after a couple of months. The office looked like wonderland by 9.00PM every night.

In truth, the only effective solution I have ever found to reduce late night work in the office was to include it in each manager's annual bonus targets. If they didn't manage their team so they were out by a set time each evening, it hit them in the bonus round. Overtime tumbled, though whether this is more a question of unreported hours rather than actual reduction in hours remained a very grey area indeed.

Cabin Fever – getting out of Tokyo

Tokyo is an awesome city. Bright lights, futuristic buildings and some thirty million people. Shinjuku station alone sees nearly four million of them each day travelling to and from their homes and offices. The city can, as a result, sometimes feel a little claustrophobic and overwhelming and when you get that feeling, you know it's time to get away.

Flying out of Japan is good for relieving stress but for a simple weekend away, it's probably a little extreme. Getting away for an overnight stay though is very simple and makes for a nice break. The issue is always one of timing. Get it wrong and your journey may be a true nightmare. Get it right and you will be in beautiful rolling countryside within a matter of an hour or two.

The main weekend break locations are accessible from western Tokyo. Hakone, Yamanakako or a little further, Karuizawa are all within two to two and a half hours drive. The key issue is when to drive and for that, Friday evening is your best idea. Leave after 8.00pm and your road will be open and clear. Leave before 7.00pm and you'll be sitting in traffic as a plug of vehicles jam their way out of the city for the weekend.

Similarly, the return journey is, if anything, even more time critical. Leave before lunch and your journey back to Tokyo will be uninterrupted. Leave after lunch and you'll be sitting in stationary traffic for several hours.

The alternative to driving is to take the shinkansen (bullet train). These are fast, efficient and always on-time. If a shinkansen is late by even a few minutes it's newsworthy, it's that rare. All shinkansen terminate at Tokyo station though Shinagawa is also useful if you are travelling southwest towards Fuji or Kyoto.

Shinkansen are predominantly pre-booked seats though there are some exceptions to this. The tickets can be bought from any main JR station, not necessarily Tokyo itself. The only issue about the shinkansen is that it can become a little pricey. A family of four travelling for a weekend to Kyoto is going to cost in the region of ¥80,000 ($800), and that's before hotel costs.

The advantage of the shinkansen is that, once aboard, you are going to have a very relaxing journey. Sit back, put your headphones on and wait for the lady with the coffee trolley.

Many expats have invested either directly or through rentals, into the *beso* market. A beso is a weekend cottage somewhere in the mountains or down by the sea. As they're out of Tokyo the price to actually buy one can become very reasonable and many people join together in small consortia and effectively time share their weekends away.

The real advantage of a beso though is that you get to keep all of your away gear there. No need to fill the car with everything you'll require for a weekend, simply keep it there and get in the car with nothing more that your jacket and wallet.

If you do decide you'd like to be the owner of a home away from home, there are two ways to go about this. You can either purchase an existing beso, often from a departing expatriate, or you can purchase the land and have one built to your own design.

Constructing a beso can take a little time, several months from start to finish, but is definitely the more rewarding approach. There are a number of companies that will assist and the main ones will have English speakers on staff to help you along. It's a good idea though to go through one that you are introduced to by another expatriate. This eliminates any problems later of the agent not being up to the job and you're left with unusable land or a half complete property.

Getting away from Tokyo for the occasional weekend is a good way to relax and see different parts of Japan. Within a couple of hours of the city you'll find great skiing in winter and good hiking in summer. And if you love the sea, surfing off the coast at Kamakura is an enjoyable way to spend a couple of days.

There are a number of different formats of hotels to try out of the city. The hotels in ski areas tend to be semi-westernized affairs designed to process people through as quickly as possible. These usually have access directly from the hotel lobby to the ski slopes. They have little atmosphere though but are functional and provide the service they are intended for, i.e. skiing.

Into the countryside the more traditional format of hotel, the *ryokan*, is more common. Ryokans will be designed in traditional style, often include an onsen and the rooms will more than likely be tatami mat rather than carpet. The style is usually a single large room where all the party will sleep together on futons.

This style of getaway can be quite entertaining with traditional food (including a multi-selection traditional breakfast) with almost everything served in the room. If you hear a knock on the door, someone will be very soon coming inside to serve you something or re-arrange your room.

Typically when you arrive you will be able to change into a light yukata or cotton dressing gown. There will undoubtedly be a fuss over the issue that foreigners are all huge, irrespective of your size, and especially large gowns and sandals will be provided. Overall, a great experience.

The only down sides of staying at a ryokan are that they remain relatively inflexible over food, service and payment. The menu will be set whether you would like something different or not. Serving a seven course breakfast is not a problem but if you ask for toast it's unlikely your request will be granted.

Additionally check-in and check-out will be at strictly fixed times, whether the room is available or whether someone else is awaiting check in or not.

The other point about ryokans that really needs addressing in this day and age is that they still charge per person. Whether there is one person in the room or four staying together, in the same room, the price will simply be a multiple of the number in the party. At ¥15,000 per person, this can be reasonable for one or two people, but add in another couple and suddenly the weekend retreat is costing ¥60,000 ($600) with the only difference being the food served, drink being charged separately, and you're all still in the same room.

Finally there is also the option of staying in a *minshuku*. These are effectively the budget rate versions of a ryokan. You will probably need to bring your own towels, there may not actually be a bath and you may end up sharing a room with a stranger. This can all be good fun if you're looking for an alternative few days but if you're looking to relax, a ryokan, despite the price, is probably the better alternative.

Essential Japanese – all you need to learn

Many new foreigners arrive in Japan with excellent intentions of learning conversational Japanese. After several months studying from "Japanese for Busy People" they eventually admit defeat and accept that they are a bilingual illiterate; someone unable to read and write in two languages.

However, even a smattering of Japanese can really make life a lot simpler. Here is a modestly short list of words that can be learnt relatively quickly to satisfy your conscience that at least you tried.

Although it may not seem so, Japanese words are pronounced without inflection, the emphasis usually being equal on all syllables. And at this point I must defer to the gross over-simplifications I'm about to use. However it will be simpler than learning the entire language and you will be basically functional.

Useful Japanese in the office:

Good morning = ohaiyo gozaimasu
Good day = konnichi wa
Good evening = komban wa
Thanks = doumo
Thank you = doumo arigatou
Thank you very much = doumo arigatou gozaimasu
Not yet = mada

Useful Japanese for directing taxis:

Right = migi
Left = hidari
Straight-on = masugu
Stop here please = kono hen de ii desu
Really stop! = Tomare!
Stop at the traffic lights = shingo de ii desu
Stop at the cross roads = kosaten de ii desu

In general usage:

I'm Bob, nice to meet you = Bob desu, yoroshiku onnegaishimasu
Please (as in "pass me something") = kudasai
Please (as in "you first") = douzo
Please (as in "do me a favor") = onnegaishimasu
Where is the XXX = XXX wa doko desu ka?
When is the XXX = XXX itsu desu ka?
Who is that? = dare desu ka?
Food = tabemono
Drink = nomimono
I want this = kore onnegashimasu
I want that = sore onnegaishimasu

Counting:

1 = ichi
2 = ni
3 = san
4 = shi
5 = go
6 = roku
7 = nana
8 = hachi
9 = kyu
10 = ju
100 = hyaku
1,000 = sen
10,000 = man

Here I am using a major generalization as there are numerous counting systems used in different circumstances, but these will get you by.

And that's about it. If you can use these few Japanese words comfortably and in context your life will become simpler. Beyond this the levels of complexity very quickly increase exponentially and it's not necessarily a problem of being able to speak Japanese but one of understanding the answer. Learn a few words, use them well and focus on understanding the country rather than the language.

Reverse culture shock – Japan wasn't so hard

The end of an expatriation to Japan cannot come soon enough for some people. In reality those are the ones who really never should have tried a secondment in the first place. Partly because they will have learnt little of what is there to be experienced both culturally and personally but also because they may well have deprived someone else from that very same learning curve. For these people, going home is probably all they've been thinking about since the day they arrived.

For the 99% of the remainder of expatriates who come to Japan, going home can lead to very mixed feelings and often this is not the end of the journey but the start of a longer one with new lands to see and friends to make. But before this, everyone goes through the process of reverse culture shock.

It is often thought of as a cliché but Japan genuinely is a polite and clean living society. Yes the trains are full, but have you ever ridden the subway at home during peak rush hour? The streets are safe, the litter is taken home and crime is almost non-existent. The greatest danger you face is getting lost and with modern smartphones this is pretty much your own fault if you can't find your way.

Going home exposes you to all the realities that were covered by rose tinted glasses when you were away. Phoning someone to ask a question is no longer an issue of language but one of getting them to pick the phone up in the first place. The streets are no longer as clean as they were and that crowd outside the bar is perhaps not as friendly and welcoming as you're used to. Reverse culture shock shows all the beliefs in the better side of your home country may not have been quite as real as you thought.

Added to this, you have changed. And by and large, everyone who has stayed at home hasn't. The same people will still be sitting in the same corner of your local cafe. They'll ask you questions for a while about "what was it like?" but soon you'll realize that they can't really comprehend what you are talking about and you begin to find yourself changing conversation without even noticing. Your first several months will be as disruptive emotionally for your family and professionally for yourself as the first months of life in Japan.

The company that first brought me to Japan, and briefly brought me back home again, was very experienced at managing global expatriations. It had a positive policy that favored those who had spent a minimum of two years overseas when it came to career prospects. Even in such a well developed program the life expectancy of a returning expatriate was less than twelve months in the same role before they looked either internally for a new assignment or to another company to send them overseas again.

Reverse culture shock will have one of two effects on you. You'll either develop a more realistic understanding of your home country and appreciation of different approaches to life, or you'll go looking for it all over again. Either way, it's a good idea to be just as prepared going home as when you leave in the first place, things are going to be different.

A Few Myths, Stories and Useful Info

The "Bubble" – the largest in history

I arrived in Japan just in time to hear people talking about the Bubble, which was bursting in slow motion all around, but was a little too late to experience its excesses. I missed the days of the million yen expense accounts and briefcases full of cash. I also missed the nights in expensive bars in Ginza being followed by a two-hour taxi home. All paid for on the company account. As I say though, they were recent enough for everyone to tell me about them.

On Tuesday, 20 October 1987, the day after Black Monday when stock markets had started to spectacularly crash around the world, the Japanese Ministry of Finance called a meeting with senior advisers, ministers and key members of the major financial institutions of Japan to discuss an appropriate response. The result was that it was agreed Japan would ignore what was happening in the rest of the world and continue to invest in the stock market, building on what was already a strong bull run. The Nikkei actually ended up in 1987, the only major market to do so.

It also ended up in 1988 finally peaking at 38,957 on 29 December 1989, some six times higher than it had been a decade before. Land was at an all time premium, the grounds of the Emperor's palace being said to be worth the same as all of California and the value of Tokyo being equivalent to all of North America. Housing was so expensive banks were offering third generation mortgages where your grandchildren would finally pay off the debt you incurred buying a small apartment.

The origins of the bubble arose when the banks had convinced the regulators that investments in land and stock should count towards their capital requirements. Effectively, the more money a bank lent to a speculator, the more the market increased and so the more money the bank had to lend. And the cycle continued, generating one of the greatest money making machines in history. Until it suddenly stopped on the last day of trading of the 1980s.

December 29, 1989 was not just the peak valuation of the stock market in Japan that year, but the peak valuation of all time. Nearly twenty five years later the Nikkei is still less than 40% of its value in 1989 and hit an all time post bubble low of 7,054 in March 2009, some 80% down after nearly twenty years.

However, unlike the bursting of other historical bubbles, such as "The Wall Street Crash" which had been characterized by explosive devaluations, the Japanese bubble burst slowly in a very controlled and Japanese way.

Unemployment remains around 5% and there are certainly a lot of Ferraris on the streets of Tokyo. The two decades following the crash, known as *the lost decades*, have been an economic catastrophe greater than that experienced during World War II, but Japan has maintained a high standard of living for its population and has worked through its problems in its own, unique way.

Market Entry – To JV or Not JV

The classical approach to market entry in Japan has been one of finding either a local Japanese distributor or establishing a joint venture with a Japanese partner. The large trading houses (*soga shosha*) such as Sumitomo, Itochu, Marubeni or Mitsui have divisions dedicated to just such business needs and until recently have provided the most common approach to establishing a presence in Japan.

For the pure green-field start up there is also the question of *how* to enter the market. This in its own right is an interesting question where perceived wisdom has been significantly altered over the last two decades. The options remain essentially the same as before however the simplicity or execution has become significantly more open following a small number of success stories in the 1990s and 2000s.

The questions that need to be asked are essentially, what will a JV partner bring to the table and will they be with me through the hard times as well as the good? Typically the trading house will provide all the facilities needed to establish a business in Japan including infrastructure, staff, necessary business licenses and business contacts. In return for this they will take a capital stake.

Many partnerships with the shosha have been very successful in the past and have provided an intermediate step to establishing a full subsidiary. However, this comes at a price. The partner will appoint key employees and when the time comes for divorce the severance agreement will be steep and the alimony will include employment for many seconded staff, whether needed or not.

Until the early 1990s the advantages of working through the shosha were considered to outweighing the disadvantages. However the key driver to making the decision still tended to be because the entrant company considered they didn't understand Japan and the shosha provided a simple and straightforward approach. *In effect, the decision boiled down to a fear of the dark.*

During the 1990's though, this perception began to change. Toys'R'Us was the first major brand to enter independently closely followed by The Gap and then Adidas, which went solo from a twenty-five year distributor relationship. Each of these demonstrated that the existing wisdom that a local partner was essential to doing business in Japan was no longer as valid as it maybe had been in the past.

For all its reputation of closed market practices and impenetrable red tape, Japan was, in fact, a very open market. To those who could understand the requirements of the Japanese consumer and were willing to make the investment for success the barriers began to disappear. Adidas identified that, by blending both international expertise and knowledge of the brand with local experience and understanding of both western and Japanese management techniques, an extremely effective business model could be developed.

However, it was also very conscious of the requirements of the Japanese consumer and established a design center to cater to their requirements. Ten years later it was a billion dollar business and the dominant player in its market sector.

These early starters demonstrated that it was possible to be successful in Japan without the support of a local joint venture partner. They were also though, very aware of the requirements to build their business and operations with reference to the requirement of the Japanese distribution model and local consumer. Although the shosha may have been of assistance in this process, these early pioneers demonstrated they weren't absolutely necessary.

The key question for a brand considering entering the market is whether, by working with a joint venture partner, is it still possible to ensure the entire organization is focused on the success of the brand.

With the best of intentions, having a senior management team with split loyalties is always going to create conflicts of interest. Unless both companies are completely aligned there will always exist a tactical or strategic difference of opinion at any one time.

Certainly in the case of Adidas, where the president personally interviewed all employees even when the business was over $500 million, one of the keys to its success was that every member of staff had an affinity for the brand and worked for its success. There is a significant question as to whether staff from a JV partner would have been as focused on the development of the brand given that they may be rotated to a new one at any time.

My opinion on this question, to JV or not JV, is very much that a JV is no longer necessary (unless required by regulation) provided the brand moves into the country with a mixed organization of not simply home country and Japanese but also foreigners who are experienced and have several years of working in Japan behind them.

These key individuals act as the bridge between the Japanese team and the head office new managers, ensuring strategies are applicable to the market and cultural confusion is kept to a minimum. A joint venture should no longer be the default mechanism to entry to Japan. It simply isn't needed anymore.

Statutory decisions – the necessary evil

The differing forms of corporate entity

When starting a business in Japan there are a number of decisions to be made. First comes the issue of what type of company to form itself. There are essentially two types of company, a GK with low administration, simpler filing but restrictions on what it can actually do.

Then there is the KK which is a full joint stock company bound only by the depth of its pockets. In certain circumstances and industries it is also possible to establish a branch entity but outside financial business these are rare.

Most serious businesses enter the market as a KK. A GK, although simpler and cheaper to operate, looks small time and few serious players would consider entering in this form. A KK has the feeling of a "real" business and banks and business partners would be looking for this form. They may be uncomfortable establishing business relations otherwise.

Although global creative tax planning may also suggest the concept of a branch office, this carries the wrong message to a market. The starting expectation is always that a new brand entering a market will be operated by foreigners who have little clue as to what they are doing and will probably close after a short period of time. To be fair this has been the case in many instances.

Entering through a branch plays to exactly these fears. It's an ethereal entity and clearly the brand isn't serious about becoming successful in the first place. It becomes a self fulfilling prophecy and most likely the brand will soon be gone having failed to develop the necessary partnerships to grow and develop the business.

How big a business do I want?

The next question is one of the size of the business and this is driven by the capital structure. Companies with share capital over ¥500m (~$5m) or with year-end liabilities of over ¥20bn (~$200m) must file audited accounts within two months of the financial year end. This audit must be signed by a Japanese qualified partner from the audit firm and must be prepared under Japanese financial regulations rather than international ones. The two being quite different in a number of respects.

As most global businesses will require a group audit under international regulations it is likely that this will become a question of two audits each year. One under home regulations and one under Japanese ones. Japanese regulations tend to be more heavily focused on tax law and hence will be unacceptable to the head office. The differences between the two sets can become a serious problem over time as the head office is unaware of the variances in rules and regulations to prepare financial statements.

This cost a certain famous oil company over $1bn as they slimmed down and exited the local expat finance director who was the only one to genuinely understand the issues at stake. Replacing him with a lower cost local finance director, the global head office was unaware that mounting FX losses were going unreported as under Japanese rules, they didn't need to be revealed. This one ended in tears.

Where possible it is possible to structure a new business so that it doesn't trigger the requirement for a local audit but can still report and be audited under international regulations. All of the large, global audit firms will provide this service.

The approach is to keep the capital under ¥500m. There is a certain start up in Japan with sales of around $1bn that has operated with share capital of ¥499m for over ten years and only triggered a local audit when liabilities exceeded ¥20bn as it grew.

This can be important as the cost of a statutory audit will very quickly exceed ¥10m ($100,000) even for modest size companies. In the above example the company saved itself this amount each year for eight years, cumulatively something in the order of $1m in cash and thousands of hours in additional workload.

The Statutory Auditor

The statutory audit should not be confused with the requirement to have a *Statutory Auditor*. Under certain, relatively common, board structures, a new company has the option to create a Board of Directors or appoint directors without a board structure. The latter is common in smaller companies and the former in larger ones. The issue with actually creating a legal Board of Directors is that it also requires the appointment of a Statutory Auditor, an internal role entirely independent of the external auditors.

In non-listed companies, the role of the Statutory Auditor could be considered akin to a Compliance Committee in western countries. Both have free reign to examine any part of the business so desired and report directly to the Board of Directors independently of any other function. The difference arises in the level of expectation.

Where as a Compliance Committee is expected to be highly experienced and qualified, independent minded individuals, the Statutory Auditor has historically simply been an almost ceremonial position. There is no professional qualification required and the individual will often have a direct personal relationship with members of the Board or potentially the Chairman. Independence is not necessarily expected.

For the purposes of foreign companies, the position of statutory auditor is therefore often held by a senior member of the head office finance team, potentially even the global CFO. They are required to sign Board minutes and resolutions but outside this have little, if no, duties to perform.

Within listed companies this is not quite the case. There is clearly a higher expectation placed on the Statutory Auditor and lapses in corporate governance can lead to them being held personally liable for failures or losses. However, the question of independence from the Board remains an open issue.

When to start the business

The next question is when to actually start business. This might seem a trivial question, as the answer should be as soon as possible. The issue here is tax planning around consumption tax. As regulations change it is always necessary to receive updated advice however it is worth looking at the first two years of business as there can be significant opportunities here.

In some circumstances it is possible to retain the actual consumption tax on sales; that's an additional 5% in your pocket. The important element here is that the rules always look at the first two financial years once sales begin. In the instance you are very close to the year-end, it is a good idea to resist the temptation to push sales in the last month and start afresh the following financial year. You've gained yourself an entire additional twelve months of an additional 5%.

Choosing a year-end

There is then also the issue of the financial year-end. Under corporate law this can be any date however the financial year must be a maximum of twelve months. Not a problem except in the instance of a change of the year end which usually needs to be executed by using a short financial year and a standard one rather than having one long one.

Staffing the team

One final point on auditors in Japan and the impact on the corporate finance team is that, whereas in the US there are over 300,000 CPA's and an equivalent number of financially qualified people in the UK, Japan has less than 20,000 financially qualified individuals. I once challenged a delegation from METI on this lack of basic resource. Their response was that "it is important to maintain quality standards" and hence they rejected the concept of more people in the market with some form of financial qualification.

This may maintain a high standard for the individuals involved but, taken on average, it significantly reduces the overall qualifications of the finance industry by forcing untrained individuals into the market. There is simply no one else to recruit. Non-Japanese speakers are not going to get far in a kanji based environment.

A Job for life – was it ever real?

There is a belief in foreign countries that in Japan, a job is for life and the individual will join, work and retire all with the same company. This has an element of truth to it but, as with all general assumptions, is also something of an urban myth.

There are companies that have operated on this basis, recruiting the young, promoting them each year as they grow older, and never considering releasing them. In return, the company expects their unquestioning loyalty and continuous hard work and efforts. However, there is a significantly larger element of the corporate economy that works on a more familiar approach of adapting their work force to the conditions at the time.

The "jobs for life" concept really only applied (note the past tense) to Tier One companies such as Toyota, Matsushita or Sumitomo. Below these companies, in the Tier Two and down, corporate life has always been a struggle and companies recruit the best they can and hold on to them as long as possible.

The workers may stay with the company or they may decide to move around (though they are unlikely to break into a tier one company from this position). The company may hire the young or the middle aged and may close departments or divisions, laying off workers in the process, as business demands.

A job for life did exist in Japan at one time, especially post war when worker loyalty was critical, but it applied to only a limited section of the economy and essentially is now a thing of the past. Even the Tier One companies have now adjusted their retention strategies and starting in the late 1990s have begun to downsize where and when necessary.

Initially this was limited to transferring employees from the main company to subsidiaries, at which point the employee would usually take the hint and look for alternative opportunities. However, from the early 2000s it became more commonplace for companies to downsize directly with both Nissan and Sony leading the way.

Just in Time – how effective is it?

Toyota became famous for inventing *Just-in-Time* inventory management. The items required for a particular step of a manufacturing process would arrive at the assembly point "just in time", that is, only at the precise moment actually needed. Almost nothing was held in inventory. As a result working capital requirements were reduced and productivity enhanced.

However, everyone else in the supply chain had to maintain inventory and in many cases, maintain warehouses for continuous replenishment very close to the Toyota factories. The actual item itself wasn't being conjured out of thin air but was being stored ready for delivery by a third party rather than by Toyota itself.

In effect, what Toyota had invented was "delegated working capital" where someone else is having to bear the cost of inventory as a condition of being a supplier to a tier one company.

The weakness of just-in-time management came to the fore following the earthquake of March 2011.

However, it had surfaced ten years earlier during the foot and mouth epidemic of 2001 in the UK. Toyota famously announced the restriction on supplies of finished models due to a "shortage of cows". The leather supply had been so severely disrupted there weren't enough cows to go around and production had to be reduced. As the process operated under the just in time philosophy, there were no stores of hides put aside for contingency purposes.

After March 2011, the existing limited inventory supplies were very quickly exhausted and many of the major manufacturers had to idle plants until supply chains could be re-established. As a result, there is now significant debate within the country as to whether just-in-time production should be modeled on something more flexible which, although less efficient, will be more resilient in the instance of another natural disaster.

Outside the major manufacturers, just-in-time inventory can carry a significant associated cost. Once a supplier has identified that a company tends to want to be able to change an order right up to the wire, they will actually produce two of each required item. The one they expect to be required and the contingency, nearly finished article, that can be adapted at the last moment to fulfill an adjusted requirement.

And you can be sure it is not the supplier that will bear the cost of this additional production. Just-in-time is an expensive process to adopt for international brands in Japan, there often isn't the critical mass to drive the efficiency required.

Not here yet? – finding a position in Japan

Working and developing a career in Japan can be immensely rewarding, however actually starting the process can be quite difficult to simply get off the ground. Let's assume you have a degree in Japanese and are fluent in the language both written and spoken, it would initially appear to be a simple task to move to Japan and find a new role. However, there is one additional issue to be faced. The visa.

If you are not a Japanese national then, to work in Japan, you will require a valid visa for the purpose. The vast majority of these come in one of two forms, a working visa sponsored by the company that will employ you, or a spouse visa giving you the right to reside and work in Japan. There are other very specific visas but these two make up the majority of the non-Japanese working population.

For someone arriving as an English teacher, the companies that recruit people for these roles are very experienced at processing the visa requirements. They will be able to assist from start to finish as their business is to bring foreigners to Japan in the first place. Outside this, companies are rarely set up to bring foreigners into Japan unless it is at a very senior level, officer or director.

Most foreigners new to working in a company in Japan will have joined the company in their home country and are then transferred internally to the Japanese operation. However, trying to apply directly to a Japanese company is a very different proposition.

There are essentially two types of company operating in Japan. Firstly, domestic companies that are pure Japanese operations and secondly, the local subsidiary of a foreign company. Domestic companies typically have a very structured approach to recruitment, especially new graduates. There are specific times of the year, in some cases down to a few days, where thousands of graduates will be interviewed and offered positions. These graduates will join the company and be assigned their future role.

It would be virtually inconceivable for a domestic company to consider bringing in a foreign graduate into this process. They are neither set up for it nor in the need of the foreign graduate when there are fewer positions than local graduates in the first place. For the prospective recruit, the approach is then usually to look to the subsidiary of a foreign company.

Foreign brands enter Japan in one of two ways, and it is important to understand which is which. The traditional approach is either through a domestic company entering into a licensing agreement or joint venture with a foreign brand or through a foreign brand entering the market directly itself. Notice that in the first instance, even if the arrangement is through a joint venture structure, this remains essentially a domestic company although there may be senior representatives from the foreign company itself. It is unlikely that this form of arrangement will look to recruit new foreigners as they can easily reach out to local talent readily available in the market.

In the 1990s, companies such as Toys R Us, The Gap and Adidas, demonstrated the new business model of direct entry into the market. This opened up the options and these entities became a hybrid of Japanese and international culture. It is potentially with companies that have taken this approach that there is the best opportunity for a starting role in Japan.

However, it remains important to look at this from the company's perspective. A foreign entity in Japan can consider multiple alternatives when hiring for junior or mid-level positions. They can hire local staff directly and if they have the correct skill set, this is the simplest and quickest approach. They could also hire Japanese graduates directly out of foreign schools who are overseas.

This has the advantage of hiring someone with both local and international skills and no barriers to language or work permits. The third alternative is to hire a foreign student and sponsoring the visa. Clearly the third option comes with greater risks for the company over the first two as well as adding a new time dimension for the visa application.

It is often cited that once a company sponsors a visa it is then liable for the actions of the individual or that the individual may abscond and take their precious work visa to a new company. Short of the sponsor actually going to the government and notifying them and having the visa revoked, there is little that can be done to prevent this happening.

However, my personal experience is that these concerns are overblown and that the real issue is all down to timing. Except in the instance of senior roles, when a company is recruiting it is usually for an already open position or one soon to become open. Having the right person fill this position as quickly as possible becomes a priority and companies are often willing to slightly compromise on fit to have a new recruit at a desk.

When reviewing the options, even when the foreign graduate is the best possible candidate there is still the visa process to complete. This may take a matter of a few weeks or a few months and ultimately may not be successful at all. The company is therefore faced with the choice of potentially compromising and bringing in a local hire who may not be perfect for the role, or waiting the extra time and taking the chance on the foreigner.

As the decision to hire a person is often heavily influenced by the manager who will have to take on the extra burden if a place is not filled, it's not hard to see why the usual outcome is for the local hire. So the reason why foreign companies do not often arrange visas for international hires has nothing to do with the talent and skill set of the individual but significantly more to do with internal requirement of the company itself.

At the end of the day there is a demand for a body at a desk. If this can be filled more quickly through a local hire then this is what is going to happen.

As such a foreigner trying to find a new position in Japan is in competition with Japanese graduates who have studied overseas and have both Japanese and international skill sets and local hires who can be available at very short notice. The key question, therefore, is how to make themselves stand out when the skill set is not the issue in question at all.

The simplest and most successful way to do this is to have patience, identify a company you want to work for in Japan, and go about getting hired in your home country. Once inside a company the opportunities increase dramatically and organized international transfers become a possibility.

Global HR departments exist to drive transfer programs. Internship opportunities are regularly circulated and the simple network connections all increase the chances for an international transfer. Looking from the company's point of view again, the person goes from being an unknown to a known. Their motivation and ability can be properly assessed and there is a catch-net in place if the transfer to Japan ultimately doesn't work out as expected.

There are effectively two approaches to this process, going through the home country head office or through the home country retail business (in the instance you choose a brand with a retail network). Of the two, retail is likely to be the quicker and simpler.

Although it may not at first appear the most desirable route, anything that brings you closer to Japan should be considered. The advantage of retail is that it provides the person with the opportunity to learn the brand, its core values, the product, the consumer, as well as be trained in sales and the store systems.

By taking the time to learn the brand they are reducing the economic risk to the company of investing in an international transfer. However, the company, although now potentially willing to sponsor the individual, is unlikely to be willing to cover additional costs of a transfer, living expenses in Japan etc.

However, a determined transferee would be willing to cover those costs anyway. The real benefit is being a known quantity, being within the corporate catch net and getting onto the radar of senior management as someone who is a risk taker but has realistic expectations of what to ask others.

Once in Japan, brands are continuously searching for bilingual staff, especially in Tokyo. A material element of retail in Tokyo is actually driven by tourists and having a foreign face in the store to ask for help from can be seen as a real benefit. So a foreigner who knows the brand, systems, processes and who is bilingual and willing to have the same contract as all the other staff in the store, becomes a value added proposition for the brand and quite desirable.

The next step is how to move from the store to the head office if this is the ultimate objective. A foreigner working in retail will quickly come to the notice of the local senior management if they weren't already on their radar. Positions in a head office do become regularly available and so again, it's a matter of patience waiting for the right opportunity, as well as having been seen to have fulfilled the original commitment of contributing to the store business as well.

Suddenly, all the negatives about being foreign, overseas, unknown and inexperienced have been addressed. They are known, proven, trained and immediately available. *The negatives have become positives.*

Moving from head office positions between countries can be more difficult and likely to take more time. Interviewing for the head office position and expressing a desire to leave to go overseas is unlikely to result in landing the position in the first place. No manager wants to hire someone today knowing they'll need to hire a new person tomorrow. An applicant will need to make a greater commitment to position in this instance.

However, assuming that this can be accommodated within a career development plan, it will provide valuable experience before transferring out again. Unfortunately times have changed in the entry-level positions and it is more probable than not that the individual will need to commit to zero additional cost to the company.

They will have to take a local contract, pay their own travel costs and expect to receive the same working conditions, including vacation days, as their co-workers. However, they will be in Japan.

The variation on a theme to this is, rather than joining an international brand and transfer to the Japanese subsidiary, consider joining a Japanese company overseas and work to being transferred back. With the rise of companies such as Rakuten or Uniqlo, which are expanding rapidly internationally and are looking for high quality foreign talent, this becomes a very real possibility. These are essentially hybrid companies, Japanese but at the same time international.

Rakuten has a stated company policy that all meetings, wherever they are held, must be held in English. When this was announced it caused the predictable shockwave in Japan but more and more companies are beginning to see "Japanese only" as a limitation to growth rather than a necessity for employment.

If the options above still do not satisfy the objectives then there is also the option of an internship as a route into Japan. Although, almost by definition, it will need to be completely self funded, by applying to international brands directly in Japan there may be the possibility of finding a short-term position that could lead to a longer one. Personal contacts are always a good approach and being known already in Japan, it will not hurt to ask directly for possible introductions. If this still isn't a viable option, then find a wonderful Japan husband or wife and make the commitment!

Olympus – what actually went wrong

The following is simply my opinion on the Olympus scandal. I make that statement in the instance lawyers become involved. And that was part of the problem. It was seen as a legal and ethical scandal. Which it was. But if the objective was to bring the house down, what actually happened was to shore up the foundations rather than undermine them. And that's because the approach taken was western rather than Japanese.

In summary this is what happened. In the fall of 2011 an English executive, Michael Woodford, was plucked from the ranks of semi-obscurity to become president and subsequently CEO of Olympus, a multi-billion dollar optics and medical appliances firm. Unbeknownst to him at the time, Olympus had been making losses over the last two decades on investments made during the Bubble and were using interesting financial structuring to hide these from investors and the public at large.

The straw that broke the camels back was the acquisition of a UK company for which the "consulting" fees were close to $700m or approximately 30% of the acquisition value. This compared to the usual 1~2% fee.

The funds were paid through a series of vehicles, primarily offshore and hard to trace, alleged shell companies. However these funds were then recycled and used to essentially cover some of Olympus's losses. Investors may question the level of the fees but would be unaware of the underlying losses being hidden.

Woodford came to be aware of this and, to cut a long story short, essentially threatened to fire the entire Board and bring in outside investigators to uncover the truth.

The Board of Olympus then called an emergency meeting, timing this for the day Woodford was in Tohoku visiting tsunami victims. The surprise arrangements forced him to promptly turn around and head back to Tokyo to attend the meeting. A meeting at which he was neither allowed to speak or vote.

He was ousted from his position as CEO and president and essentially sent packing with the rationale that he didn't fit in with the corporate culture. Not bad after a few weeks in the role.

Calling on the major investment funds to back him in cleaning up the company and re-establishing a completely new Board of Directors, he received not a single vote from the Japanese institutional funds, which make up the majority shareholders in the company. Realizing the game was up, Woodford resigned from the company and returned to the UK to commence a law suit for damages relating to his, now curtailed, four year contract.

The share price of Olympus during this time naturally took a substantial hit and with a straight face, the new president of the company made a press statement that *"if the secret information had not been leaked, there would have been no change in our corporate value"*.

Ultimately the top executives of Olympus were arrested and charged with various degrees of accounting fraud. The maximum sentence handed down eventually being one of a three year suspended jail sentence. This compared to imprisonment for UK MP's for fiddling a few thousand pounds in expenses (and quite right too).

What Woodford did wrong (in my opinion) was to approach this in a western way. It would appear he completely forgot about nemawashi. The objective was to come clean to investors and public alike of the details of the situation and to ensure it would not happen again by replacing the Board or, at a minimum, making it independent of the executive of the company.

Woodford issued the equivalent of an open letter, and considering the number of people who were copied, it may as well have been published in a newspaper. He stated the case correctly and then on the final page made clear his intention to replace the key individuals and, by using a broad circulation, effectively threw the gauntlet at their feet. He then left Tokyo and allowed events to take their course. Which, of course, they did.

An alternative approach, whilst keeping the key objectives of transparency and reform in mind, would have been to take this individually to each of the key players. Talk them through and ensure they were very clear on his sincerity and determination to ensure the best for the company, investors and employees and to uphold the legal and ethical standards demanded of each of them. He should have gained at least their tacit agreement to this and requested their support, or even assistance, in the process.

By approaching the issue in this way, the Japanese rather than western way, Woodford would have maximized his chances of achieving his objectives. This whilst potentially remaining in his position to champion further corporate governance reforms for the Japanese market.

Instead it was all a bit of an embarrassment that cost everyone their positions. It also possibly didn't go as far as it could have whilst at the same time tainting every foreign executive in Japan with the reputation of a loose canon. Ultimately it could be argued that this has set back Japan's internationalization by creating a moment of hesitation to bring outsiders into the family. When in Rome....

MOF-tan – something for the old resume

By the mid-1990s the "Bubble" in Japan had well and truly burst. The economy was suffering and the major banks and corporate institutions suffering along with it. More and more financial scandals were being uncovered especially in the instance of *tobashi*, the practice of using Japanese accounting regulations to hide losses by keeping them in subsidiaries or offshore institutions.

In those days there was no requirement to prepare consolidated accounts and so hiding losses was relatively straightforward. That is until LTCB, Yamaichi Securities, Takugin and a number of other financial institutions went under as a result of these undeclared losses.

In a wonderfully Japanese aside, when there was a run on Chiyoda Securities, desperate investors queued through the streets to recover their funds. The queues though were very orderly, everyone being issued with a number to be called forward in turn.

The Ministry of Finance (MOF) was now under pressure to do something and so had upped the ante in public and started a process of random and unannounced bank audits and inspections. This went well with the general public who were seeing the financial institutions being brought under some form of control.

However, it wasn't too well received by the institutions themselves who did not appreciate a squad of inspectors turning up without notice at their door.

As a result the banks created internal departments referred to as *MOF-tan* with the sole responsibility of pumping MOF officials for information about inspections and other useful policy directions. Their approach was extremely effective; get to know the official, take him out regularly to hostess bars, get him drunk, get him to talk.

The MOF-tan budgets could be significant with some of the subsequent reports showing hundreds of thousands of dollars being lavished on individual government officials.

The MOF-tan departments essentially exploded in the mid to late 1990s as they became more of an embarrassment to the banks than an asset. However, still, it must have been quite a time while the party lasted.

Crime – who you are or what you did?

Let's look at two recent examples of white-collar crime in Japan. Livedoor and aforementioned Olympus.

In the case of Livedoor, the company was an internet startup from the mid-1990s that rode the wave of the tech bubble very effectively to create an enormous web services company by the early 2000s. With over a thousand employees and offices in the prestigious Roppongi Hills district of Tokyo, it could have been considered a major success story for the Japan tech industry.

However in 2006 rumors started to circulate that there had been inconsistencies in the company's finances where they were alleged to have been cooking the books. Eventually the house of cards fell and the charismatic figurehead of the company was sentenced to two and a half years jail time for fraud and false accounting to the tune of several tens of millions of dollars.

In the case of Olympus, over a period of more than two decades, the company fraudulently covered losses through financially manipulating offshore subsidiaries and paying several hundred million dollars in fees. Not only did shareholders lose through these transactions, when the scandal became public they lost several billion dollars more as the share value collapsed. The result, suspended sentences all round.

The difference between Olympus and Livedoor and the resulting inverted sentencing should be left to the lawyers to debate. But the general feeling in the business community in Japan is that, if you are going to do something questionable, don't be young, wear a jumper or appear on TV shows. Unless you like jail.

Déjà vu – Japanese TV commercials

One of the surprising things for a new foreigner to Japan is the quality, or better put, the style, of Japanese TV commercials. Aside from a few that are genuinely witty (such as the Nissin Cup Noodles which are hysterical) most appear to follow one of two formats. Shouting about the product or presenting something cute about the product. The name is repeated multiple times and the whole event is over in 15 seconds.

Then something interesting occurs. The commercial is immediately repeated all over again. Unchanged and unrepentant, the product name is once again shouted from the screen. It took me many years to work out that these two issues, the lack of creativity and the repetition, are actually two sides of one coin.

In Japan it is the access to TV broadcasting, rather than the content of the commercial, that is the barrier to entry. To air a commercial it is necessary to go through one of the few dominant media resellers. Once you are past them, it doesn't matter so much the actual content as you are finally into the living room.

As the shortest TV commercial spot available is 15 seconds it's more economic to make a short commercial and show it twice if you are lucky enough to gain a 30 second slot than to go to the expense of making an entirely new commercial or a 30 second version of the first.

For this reason many foreign brands tend to downplay the usage of terrestrial TV and focus more on digital marketing. Often the solution to this is to import an expatriate as the marketing director and have a good, locally staffed team supporting them. It's not something that will be resolved overnight though.

The few and far between – foreigners at the helm

The corporate market in Japan remains remarkably insular when it comes to foreign ownership or foreign management. You could count on the fingers of one hand the number of foreign presidents there have been of major Japanese corporations.

Carlos Ghosn made a spectacular success of the turn around of Nissan. Brought in to Japan in the late 1990s to run a failing brand, Nissan was close to collapse losing several billion dollars in the year he arrived. Renault, its French partner had acquired slightly under 40% of the automaker when it was at its lowest ebb and brought Ghosn in as COO to turn the business around.

Initially the public (including myself it has to be said) was extremely skeptical as to whether the brand could be salvaged and secondly whether a foreigner could be the one to do this. Ghosn proved the skeptics wrong and within a few years had created one of the most profitable automotive companies in the world.

The changes he made were ground breaking for the Japanese market but he had two trump cards to play. Firstly, Nissan was broke. Without a friendly take over it was soon going to collapse, the banks unwilling to continue to support such dead weight. This made the Nissan management more open to new ideas and change than would otherwise have been the case. Secondly, he had the full support of the Renault Board and therefore felt relatively secure in his role.

The first change he made was to address the keiretsu structure of the business. This structure, where the work and orders are farmed out to group companies on the basis of trying to be "fair to everyone" had ensured that the group suppliers had been held above water but at the cost of fatally weakening the core business.

Ghosn took everyone to an offsite for the weekend and explained that this was no longer going to be the case. Orders would be fulfilled on commercial terms and there were to be no exceptions. Essentially he cut the life-lines for a large portion of the traditional suppliers of Nissan. But if he hadn't, there wasn't going to be much of a business left to supply.

There was a huge outcry in the press but Ghosn stuck to his guns and pushed the changes through. And Nissan saw it's first profit in many a year. The public outcry went on "mute" mode as people began to take a more "sit back and see" approach. Perhaps this man knew what he was doing after all.

Ghosn continued with a series of innovations, including closing domestic production, ending unprofitable models and heavily investing in an entire new range. The new GT-R was developed to show just what the company was capable of. Nissan was back on its feet.

There was one hiccup in the process but the PR people at Nissan must be given huge credit for how they handled the situation. Ghosn lived in central Tokyo and tended to drive himself around, another innovation for the president of a Japanese automotive company. One day, fairly close to his apartment building in Moto-Azabu, he was involved in a minor traffic accident.

This wouldn't have been an issue had he not been driving his Porsche at the time. Not a great image for the president of Nissan. The PR people responded to press enquiries extremely creatively though. "He had been product testing another brand and clearly it wasn't up to the job".

Carlos Ghosn's tenure at Nissan has to be seen as one of the outstanding successes of a foreigner at the center of Japanese corporate culture. There really haven't been any others quite as spectacular but there has been another notable one.

Howard Stringer, a Welsh born American citizen was brought into Sony after a successful thirty year career at CBS in the US. He joined through the media side of the business following a successful career in television and production.

Sony was not the shining star it once had been and in 2005 Stringer inherited a company that had somewhat lost its way. It had been late to the computer party, introduced a series of unwanted technologies such as MD followed by Hi-MD and was squaring up to be an also-ran in the flat screen TV market.

The corporate culture of continuously evolving into new markets was a millstone on the profitability of the existing businesses. A single major failure in the film business would have had been disastrous for the entire organization. But it did have one shining jewel and that was the Play Station. It was a money machine of unimaginable proportions.

Stringer's appointment came as a surprise in the Japanese market. To say he was relatively unknown would be an understatement. By 2013 when he retired, on the face of it his tenure could be seen with a large question mark hanging over it. However, considering the situation he inherited in 2005, simply keeping the business afloat should be seen as an achievement.

In 2003 Sony had shocked the markets by announcing profits more than $1bn short of prior forecasts. A global restructuring was enacted leading to a feeling of a re-active approach rather than a pro-active one. Confidence in the entire electronics sector in Japan was shaken and the markets tumbled. This became known, somewhat unfairly, as *The Sony Shock*. And it was in the light of this that Howard Stringer was bought in to resurrect a once great brand.

Stringer realized that the company was heavily dependent on a silo mentality and that, during the period of reconstruction, it had lost a the flare and innovation it was once known for. Perhaps he acted a little too slowly but by his retirement Sony was beginning to show signs of a recovery of imagination. New products are in the pipeline with the drive into shutterless camera technology a good example.

The interesting question will be whether this is a move into technical excellence, a la Betamax, or a move into commercial excellence, a la Samsung. Howard Stringer may not have been entirely successful in his desire to re-ignite the excitement of the brand, but at least Sony is still here and lives to fight another day.

The interesting issue about Stringer's replacement is that initially it was seen as yet another regression of a Japanese firm trying a foreigner at the helm and deciding to return to a local president instead. This perception couldn't be further from the truth though.

Kazuo Hirai was appointed to the CEO position in his early fifties, something of a surprise for most Japanese firms where the annual progression tends to determine who is in line for the top positions. However, the really interesting point comes from his early days.

Hirai was educated at The American School in Japan, an English language, international syllabus school taught predominantly by American and international teachers. Hirai is the forerunner of the international generation, one that is comfortable in all environments whether Japanese or foreign. Sony didn't replace Stringer with a *local*, they replaced him with an *international*.

Extreme Crisis Management

Following the earthquake and subsequent nuclear crisis of March 2011 there was significant debate within the business community of Japan as to how different companies responded and what should have been best practice.

Some companies insisted at the time that the foreigners leave the country. Some offered evacuation to all staff, irrespective of whether they were foreigners or local hires. Some relocated staff to Osaka, 500 kilometers (300 miles) to the west whilst others stayed and continued to operate from Tokyo.

There were no right or wrong answers to the approach to the crisis however the general agreement was that there were certain principles that companies could consider when planning for a crisis.

Reviewing events unfold, there had been one of the largest earthquakes in history followed by a tsunami that peaked at thirty eight meters (140 feet), followed by a nuclear crisis followed by power blackouts, widespread transport disruption and very quickly gasoline and food shortages.

No disaster recovery plan was ever going to be able to address this series of events however it is possible to apply a basic set of guidelines, a framework to work within.

The following were the concepts we either applied at the time or adopted as the situation progressed. One key issue though is that, whatever the checklist or disaster recovery plan you may have in place, there is no substitution for old-fashioned common sense and the application of a moral compass. Sometimes you don't have time to refer to a manual.

One important aspect of crisis management to remember is that you don't need a M9.0 earthquake to find yourself with a major crisis on your hands. The outbreak of SARS in Asia came within days of closing down major commercial hubs. Floods in Thailand or even Europe caused massive disruption as did the riots in England when civil unrest closed city centers across the country for a few days over summer 2011. Indeed, volcanic activity in Iceland disrupted transatlantic business for over a week in 2010 causing the largest closure of European airspace since WWII.

The key issue is that disasters happen in all shapes and sizes, ours just happened to be an excellent training program for how to cope with the next one.

Prepare

As discussed, it isn't realistic to prepare for all eventualities but you can very easily cover the basics. Do you know who is in charge at the time of a crisis. Potentially the management team is off-site or injured.

Do you have a group email address that covers ALL employees, including interns and short-term assignees? You will need to communicate decisions and it is easy to miss entire sections of a company if a distribution list is incomplete or not designed to be comprehensive.

Do you have a bilingual communication system in place to notify staff of decisions and actions? Email is the simplest however what is the back-up plan if the server room has lost power and the email system is off-line.

Have you tested your communication system to ensure the message will get through? Cascade a mail to the entire company and ensure everyone receives it. Test it early on a Saturday morning and measure the results. Follow up on any identified failures.

Have you tested your building evacuation plans? How would you confirm that the building is empty and where should staff go once they have exited the building?

Do you know how to create a phone call to multiple people? Do you have a crisis team that is empowered to manage in this situation? Physical meetings may become impossible and in that instance, test how you would organize a teleconference with the senior team to decide the necessary action steps. Indeed the telephone system may not work at all so do you have Skype details or some other internet based system?

None of this basic preparation steps represent a significant expense and all are relatively easily organized. Annually test your plans under real world conditions, choose a Friday afternoon and tell the staff to exit the building assuming there had been an earthquake and make their way home assuming the transport systems were down.

In doing so you address a number of issues including remembering to keep comfortable footwear and warm clothes in the office and know how to walk home and which way to go. On March 11, many didn't know the way home; remember for many of them, transport has always been underground.

People first

The safety of your staff and their families is paramount. The first actions of a management team should be to ensure they are safe and unhurt and render assistance where needed as quickly as possible.

Treat people equally. If evacuation is necessary, offer it to all the staff and not just the foreigners. The option of evacuation will only be taken up by a limited number of employees but the tension and stress levels of everyone will be reduced. Don't forget temporary staff as well. In principle their own companies should look after them but if they have been with you a long time, they are ethically part of your team.

The alternative to treating all employees as equals and offering evacuation only to the foreign staff on cost grounds is morally questionable and will have a negative impact on management's ability to operate and the general credibility of the foreigners in the future. The business will resume at some point and it will be necessary for everyone to be able to work together which means everyone must be treated equally at the time of crisis. It's simply the right thing to do.

Communicate

As a senior management team, even if you have nothing to say, it is reassuring for the employees to receive regular communications and updates. A daily update to staff suffering power blackouts, aftershocks or worse, of even basic information has a significant impact on morale. It generates a feeling that the management team is there, that they are doing something and that someone is in control.

If possible this should start the day of the crisis, although it is not always possible to identify the scale of the event. At a minimum start the day after continue until events have returned to relative stability ensuring all written communications are bilingual.

Remember communication has to be bilingual. It may be ok to send an English message to a limited audience but this is a time of crisis, it shouldn't be made harder for anyone simply because of language ability. If possible also place the communication on a Facebook page so that people have the chance to comment, they may still need help and this is a good method to organize it.

There will also be a significant level of communication from the global business in the instance of a foreign brand. Establish a single point of contact between the global and Japan teams for all key decisions and discussions.

In reality this should be two people in each location, with one primary and one backup, in the case of emergency. Backups should always confirm they have, or will, update the primary contact as soon as possible. Managing in a crisis is complex and fluid and having clear and un-contradictory decisions may be key to safety and recovery.

Be flexible

In the middle of a crisis it may not be possible to follow policies or company rules. Common sense must ultimately rule the day. Ensure all necessary parties are aware of this and where necessary empower the management to act as necessary.

If applicable, ensure decision authority is devolved from the global head office to the local one. Clearly notify the key personnel in each department of their new authorization levels. This becomes important as these people may not be experienced in taking the necessary acts on their own authority that may be critical.

The last thing that is needed in the middle of a major crisis is someone pulling out a rulebook and saying they can't do something as it's against policy. Common sense is now policy.

Act quickly

Be fast in making and communicating decisions. Delays can lead to greater hardship and possibly even compromise employee safety. At the time of a crisis it is not a localized crisis to a single company but rather one affecting millions of people.

Rapidly taking decisions such as announcing the office will be closed for a period of time allows staff to focus on their families instead. Reserving hotel rooms may provide a lifeline to staff that have lost homes. It will make a significant difference to the staff themselves and the morale of everyone in general.

The danger of delay is that your options are closing down around you. Announce the office is closed too late and half your staff may already be on the way to work. By now it's too late to ensure a complete flow of communication and now you've added to the work list by requiring to send someone to meet everyone at the office and tell them it's closed. You also have to contact that person and they may have a severely disrupted journey themselves and so it goes on.

When the earthquake struck in Tohoku we started to discuss the option of opening a relief office in Osaka, 500km west of Tokyo, for staff who would prefer not to remain. I confirmed with our corporate real estate company the possibilities and there were several options available. That was in the morning. When I called back in the afternoon all options were no longer available. By discussing for a number of hours we had missed the opportunity. And we had wasted several hours of discussion and alignment with head office. By not being nimble enough, we had created additional work at a time we really didn't need anymore.

Stay positive

The crisis of March 2011 started on Friday 11 and escalated over the following week. Rumors of radiation clouds laying waste to Tokyo or Fuji erupting and leveling the cities around became all too common and the television provided nothing but twenty-four hour coverage of the devastation.

All of this can begin to make even the most seasoned manager begin to be concerned. The important point is that if the management team shows this concern or worse signs of panic it becomes amplified throughout the rest of the company.

Staying positive is important and it may be the difference between a functioning or failing team. Avoid watching the news reports twenty-four hours a day; the crisis has happened, if there's a new development you will hear about it.

In a leadership position the entire company is looking to you as a leader to lead. They need to be reassured that someone is working to resolve the issues being faced and that they genuinely believe the situation will improve. They need to hear positive sounds, even if the message does not carry positive news.

Keep calm and carry on

The crisis of March 2011 was unique in that it was not a single event but multiple unraveling disasters happening over a period of time. The loss of Fukushima not only created an unparalleled nuclear disaster, it also disrupted the power supplies to northern and eastern Japan. As a result of this, not only did Tokyo become dark as people saved power but the transport system became unreliable meaning that people found it would take many hours to commute to and from work.

The normal life that everyone was used to no longer existed and people had to rapidly adapt to the new situation. This is extremely stressful for everyone involved and it will become important to look for signs of stress within the staff. Some people will accommodate a crisis better than others, some may not be able to cope at all.

Consider offering counseling on an anonymous basis if this becomes an issue, especially for the staff who have been more directly involved and may have witnessed the disaster first hand such as being caught in a tsunami or having lost family members.

Additionally don't forget to watch for signs of stress in yourself as well. The sleepless nights from continuous aftershocks and constant pressure will take a physical toll on everyone including yourself. *Crises are just that, a series of events beyond your control. However they do not need to become self-inflicted catastrophes.*

Crisis Preparation Checklist – BEFORE the crisis

1) An email distribution list exists for ALL employees
   a. It includes all non-head office employees
   b. It includes all brands or subsidiaries
   c. It includes temp staff
   d. It includes relevant non-employees including Group visitors
   e. It includes staff in remote locations

2) The Crisis Team has been appointed
   a. It includes the people to facilitate communication
   b. It includes a single point of contact for global business
   c. It has a communication system for meetings and calls
   d. It has an emergency Facebook page

3) Communication systems have been tested
   a. The Crisis Team have successfully tested communications with ALL current members
   b. All relevant communications were bilingual
   c. The test of the "all employee email communication" was received by all employees
   d. The Crisis Team updated the Facebook page

e. The communication systems have been tested bi-annually

4) Evacuation procedures have been tested
   a. Staff had appropriate footwear and apparel for a journey home on foot
   b. Staff knew how and where to walk home
   c. Staff left promptly following the test announcement
   d. The test has been performed annually

5) The principles of crisis management are understood by the Crisis Team
   a. People first
   b. Communicate
   c. Be flexible
   d. Act quickly
   e. Stay positive

One Expat Working in Japan

As discussed, arriving in Japan can seem at times to be very much akin to having landed on Mars. But it isn't necessarily the case that you either need to experience it in this way, nor broadcast it to the world that your pressure suit is holding, but only just. Japan is different but then again, what did anyone expect when they signed up for a stint on the ground. If you were looking to gain experience in America, signing up for California would have been a better option.

Over the years the single biggest failure of expatriates working in Japan that I have seen has been the question of not being prepared for what is in store. This is not necessarily suggesting learning fluency in the language and studying ancient history before leaving a home country. It is much more associated with the state of mind of being ready and prepared for anything that may be thrown at you. Yes, the language is different and yes, so is the food, the housing, the travel, the expectation, the history etc etc. And now time to move on.

Many expatriates arriving in Japan for the first time will have the advantage of a significant life support eco-system around them. They may not realize it but having a bilingual assistant is already a huge benefit to them. And if they don't recognize this, try sending the assistant on vacation for a couple of weeks and see how you get on without them. Many foreigners though arrive without this support and have to learn for themselves. This is infinitely harder but also leads to a much steeper learning curve. However both are going through the same process, simply at different speeds.

Japan is a learning opportunity and one that leaves a life long impact on those who experience its positives and peculiarities. The typical expat will develop a curiosity for everything around them that may not have been a skill before but will be invaluable in the future.

My decision to remain long term in Japan came when I had finished my first secondment here. I had been in Japan over three years, made every mistake a gaijin could, developed friendships with people I couldn't speak to and come to respect view points from all around the world. I'd come to realize that in this microcosm there was a new nationality that I hadn't experienced before; that of the international. I had also me my future wife and despite our different cultures and lack of native language ability, I realized we could communicate better together than I could with many back home.

With very much mixed feelings I realized the end of my contract had arrived and I returned to my home country and head office to be assigned to a grade of one in five hundred in an office of five thousand and at a grade of one amongst five hundred. Having been the only person at my level for over three years, and very much the only one who spoke English, I found adapting to my new environment just as much of a challenge as when I'd first arrived in Japan.

The day I made my decision to return to Japan came after less than a year though and it came in a single sentence. My new manager said to me "You've been out of the UK for more than three years, you just don't know what the world is all about". And I quit. It was important for me to return to my home country for that time, to live through the reverse culture shock and the closed attitude to different experiences. I realized that there was a place I preferred to be that would be a greater experience if I was willing to take the risk and move back to Japan. And that was nearly twenty years ago.

I love my home country and I also love my adopted country but I know where the greater experiences and opportunities lie for me. Japan will open you up to realizing your most basic character faults but also your unknown character strengths and if you can live with that, you'll have the greatest of times.